FAYETTEVILLE
NORTH CAROLINA

FAYETTEVILLE
NORTH CAROLINA
AN ALL-AMERICAN HISTORY

EMILY FARRINGTON SMITH

THE
History
PRESS

Published by The History Press
Charleston, SC 29403
www.historypress.net

Postcard on back cover courtesy of www.cardcow.com.

First published 2011

Manufactured in the United States

ISBN 978.1.60949.184.0

Library of Congress Cataloging-in-Publication Data

Smith, Emily Farrington.
Fayetteville, North Carolina : an all-American history / Emily Farrington Smith.
p. cm.
Includes bibliographical references.
ISBN 978-1-60949-184-0
1. Fayetteville (N.C.)--History. I. Title.
F264.F28S64 2011
975.6'373--dc22
2011003221

For my grandpa, Michael Farrington, who was old enough to have been an eyewitness to most of these events and whose individual viewing hours kept the History Channel in business. He missed this publication by just a few short months. Fayetteville lost a good man.

CONTENTS

Acknowledgements 11

Introduction 13

I. EARLY SETTLERS

The Cape Fear River 15

Settlers 16

Scottish Influence 17

Cross Creek 18

The American Revolutionary War 22

The War Finds Cumberland County 24

Flora MacDonald 25

A Story of the Revolution 27

Cornwallis 27

II. FAYETTEVILLE'S GOLDEN AGE

The Era of Fayetteville 31

All the News That's Fit to Print 35

The Fayetteville Independent Light Infantry 36

Education 38

Gold 40

CONTENTS

The Fayetteville Postal Service   41

Transportation   42

Fayetteville & Western   43

The *Fayetteville Observer*   45

Churches   45

The Town House/Marketplace   50

The Marquis Visits Fayetteville   53

The Good Old Days   57

III. THE GREAT FIRE OF 1831

The Town Burns   59

IV. ANTEBELLUM FAYETTEVILLE

Commerce   67

Farming   69

Banking   70

Politics   74

The End of an Era   75

V. THE CIVIL WAR

Wartime   77

Fayetteville's War Effort   80

Sherman   81

VI. RECONSTRUCTION

Fayetteville Remembers   89

Recession   93

Fayetteville Loses Its Charter   94

Fayetteville Railroads   95

Quirky Musings Worthy of Note   97

The African American Way of Life   98

Hospitals   100

Industry   102

VII. A New Century, A New Legacy
Floods   109
The Clarendon Bridge   111
World War I   113
Fort Bragg   114
Soldiers' Compassion   117
Population   118
The Stock Market Crashes   121
Farming and Textiles   122
A Visit from the First Lady   125
The Veterans' Hospital   126

VIII. Fayetteville and the Second World War
Mobilization of Fort Bragg   129
The Fayetteville and Fort Bragg Relationship   130
Wartime Efforts   133
Cumberland County Veterans   134
Life After War   134

Epilogue: Fayetteville Today and Tomorrow   137
Bibliography   139
About the Author   143

ACKNOWLEDGEMENTS

Dear Fayetteville,

I have you and only you to thank for these pages, for without you this book would be blank. These stories are merely words strung together, sentences connected through turn of phrase, paragraphs painstakingly constructed in the back corner of the library archives every Monday. The words I chose come to life only because you exist; you were the land on which these events happened.

This city is a collected body of good, hardworking, spirited individuals who strive to maintain a way of life that has been lived for centuries, a way of life that gives freely, appreciates wholly and truly embraces the southern ideal.

I thank you earnestly for being as amazing as you are.

Special thanks to my husband, Ash, and son, Bennett, for their undying support and encouragement (and the mornings they let me sleep in); my parents, Sally and Dave (who taught me everything I know); my sisters, Molly and Hana (for your endless hours of babysitting); my Aunt Beth (who will note that I did not use the word ethereal in the entire text, except for just now—promise kept); Momma Sherri and Rick for keeping me sane; and Cyd and Zach for all their help with Ben during my visit.

To my incredible friends Elie Jones, Jess Ross and Jody Westing: we're soul sisters who are eternally looking at the same star. Thanks for being the most amazing girls, the most supportive friends and the prettiest encouragers around. I don't know what I would do without you.

Many thanks also to Jess Berzon at The History Press; Larry Tew from the Fayetteville Historical Society; Ms. Hunter, Ms. Campbell and Ms. Williams at the Headquarters Library State and Local History Room; Kim Andersen Cumber at the North Carolina State Archives; and Marc Barnes. You all are fantastic!

I should also thank my grandpa again. His reaction when I told him I was writing a book was priceless: he handed me a dictionary and said, "Here. Your entire book is in there. Some assembly required, of course."

Sincerely yours,
Emily

INTRODUCTION

To envision Fayetteville, North Carolina, is to see a city steeped in culture and rich history set amongst modern marvels and a thriving economy. Nearly 250 years ago, John Newberry built a modest gristmill on Cross Creek, and that's what started it all. As the farthest inland port on the Cape Fear River, Fayetteville began growing as a center of commerce and trade. Today, a modernized dam stands in place of Newberry's mill, lying in the cool shadows of Fayetteville's tallest buildings.

Fayetteville city planners have done an exceptional job of bringing in new businesses to the downtown area while still maintaining the charm of an early mill town. Today, one can find banks, shops and restaurants nestled between churches built in the 1830s and landmarks that predate the Revolutionary War.

The following pages make a modest attempt at providing you with a crisp account of our humble beginnings: from the fledgling town of Cross Creek to the modern military acropolis of Fayetteville and Fort Bragg; from the signing of the Liberty Point Resolves to a day-to-day operation of fighting for our freedom; from fire and strife to glory and success.

My hope is that after reading, you will have a better understanding and greater appreciation for the hard work and tireless effort of our ancestors and their selfless acts to make this city what it is today: a southern gem in a world where you're hard-pressed to find one.

Perhaps great Fayetteville historian John Oates described his city best when he wrote:

> *I love the spot at the river's bend,*
> *Where the plains fall back and the hills begin,*
> *Where the pines climb high to the sun-kissed sky,*
> *And life is worth the living.*

I

EARLY SETTLERS

E very story has its beginning, but only one begins under the shady pine, beside the lazy banks of Cross Creek, beneath a Carolina sun that shines golden. Fayetteville has such a beginning. From the start, the land thrived and people stayed. The rest...well, the rest glows as bright as that sun.

THE CAPE FEAR RIVER

The story of Fayetteville wouldn't exist without the Cape Fear River, so that's where this story begins. The river connects the port city of Wilmington with the very heart of North Carolina, and it was on that river that early explorers set out to determine if its banks were livable.

North Carolina's first permanent settlers arrived in the area about the year 1650, with explorations of the Cape Fear River beginning in 1662. Little explanation is needed for how the Cape Fear got its name. At the mouth of the river lie shoals that stretch twenty miles out to sea, with high waves, sandbars and geysers that shoot water into the sky with incredible force. Throw pirates into the mix, and the river really became a place of fear, but explorers held strong and continued up the river. When the land (what is now Wilmington, North Carolina) was deemed suitable for agriculture, people began to settle down. By 1700, there were approximately four thousand settlers in the North Carolina coastal region of Albemarle, spreading westward up the Cape Fear River.

The river provided, at the time of its discovery, 150 miles of inland passages navigable by shallow-draft boats. Because of this accessibility, the Cape Fear River was a major artery of trade and travel for going on two hundred years. The stretch of the river that ran through what would become Cumberland County also contained thirty offshoot waterways, accessible by rafts and small watercraft. Perhaps the most important of these streams and creeks are what would later be called Rockfish Creek and the Lower Little River. These two creeks produced enough water pressure to turn water mills, determining that there was enough power to mill flour or things of that nature. These mills were a definite attraction to settlers, solidifying Cumberland County's place in colonial North Carolina's economy.

As it were, Fayetteville's history has essentially been shaped by the Cape Fear River and its many, many offshoots and tributaries. Had it not been for the navigability of these waterways, explorers' willingness to travel them and the energy produced by its water pressure, perhaps the area now known as Fayetteville never would have been established.

SETTLERS

Information on early settlers would not be complete without touching on the lives of indigenous tribal groups. American Indians first cultivated this land, settling the Sandhills area as early as 12,000 BC. Historians have associated Native Americans in the area with the language group known as the Siouans, identifying dozens of other tribes—such as the Cheraw, Waxhaw, Waccamaw, Croatan, Tuscarora and Cherokee—within a hundred-mile radius of Cumberland County. Today, North Carolina officially recognizes eight tribes and has the largest American Indian population of any state east of the Mississippi River.

There is no evidence (either documented or archaeological) that Native Americans had already settled this immediate area during the time of European exploration. However, there is evidence in the outlying areas. As early as AD 1500, historians have been able to date activity in the area as so-called sophisticated agriculture, where the American Indians planted defined rows and grew crops of corn, beans and many varieties of squash.

Evidence of hunting, fishing and gathering has also been found. While traditional villages or settlements have never been discovered, there certainly is evidence of life before European settlers came to the Cross Creek area.

Today, the county's present population of Native Americans exceeds four thousand people associated with the Lumbee or Tuscarora tribes. Little else is known about any relationship between local native peoples and European settlers.

SCOTTISH INFLUENCE

In the 1730s, for both economic and political reasons, Scots fled their home country and began settling in the Cape Fear region in droves. To this day, the Cumberland and Cross Creek areas still have an overwhelming Scottish presence.

In Scotland, what has been called the Highland Evictions began taking place in the 1700s and continued on into the early nineteenth century. A combination of the Highlanders' defeat by the British at the Battle of Culloden in April 1746, harsh action of the British Parliament against Scottish clans after that defeat and citizens being forced out of their homes so that their land could be used to raise sheep made life in Scotland almost unbearable. Those not forced from their land faced nearly impossible spikes in taxes and land rents.

Luckily for those native Scotsmen, Gabriel Johnston (royal governor of North Carolina and a Scot himself), offered land at low prices and convinced the legislature to offer ten years of tax-exempt status for new settlers to the area. This encouragement brought Scots from the Argyll and Bute regions of Scotland (also called Argyllshire) to the Cape Fear region. At first they arrived in small numbers; however, with the onset of the American Revolution, the migration numbers swelled in such a way that the British Crown became alarmed at Scotland's dwindled population.

Coming over on June 6, 1739, the first Scots to settle in this area were known as the "Thirty-Niners." They arrived on September 23, 1739, aboard a ship called the *Thistle*. Bringing with them their own cultural nuances, they also brought practical knowledge, like farming techniques. Farms popped up in the surrounding countryside, with crops such as corn, legumes, oats, wheat, potatoes and tobacco. Of the roughly twenty people who initially accepted Governor Johnston's tax-exemption offer, many of their family names are still present in today's community (like Bain, Campbell, McAllister, McDonald, McLean, McLeod and McPhearson). Consequently, to this day the Cape Fear Valley region of the state is still referred to as the "Land of the Macs."

Local historian Roy Parker Jr. wrote of the Scottish immigrants in his book *Cumberland County: A Brief History*. He said that "so rapid was the stream of settlement in the backcountry that by 1750…the area that was to become Cumberland was sprinkled with scores of farms and pastures. The big waterwheels of a few gristmills and sawmills were turning; a few merchants operated rough warehouse-stores at strategic locations." Some even worked in the naval stores industry, the largest industry of the day.

Even in their new home, the Scots spoke Gaelic. Ministers conducted church services in Gaelic and English, young children recited hymns and religious songs in their native tongue and the town even had a printer who produced all of his books in Gaelic. They continued to wear kilts and do their very best to maintain their clan system of Scotland.

A small settlement popped up along Rockfish Creek, creating a trading path down the lower Cape Fear. Along these paths came a solid stream of people looking for gold and cultivable land. This led to the formation of Cumberland County and incorporated cities along the Cape Fear.

CROSS CREEK

Cumberland County and the town of Cross Creek were both established in 1754. Originally part of Bladen County, Cumberland County split off because of a political division. The county assumed its name in honor of William Augustus, Duke of Cumberland and English commander at the Battle of Culloden—no doubt this decision was swayed by the immense number of Scots in the area. Cross Creek was established when a Quaker from Pennsylvania developed one hundred acres of land along Cross Creek. His name was John Newberry, and he built a gristmill and tavern right on the banks. He sold lots for houses, stores, shops and a tannery, which were the beginnings of the small community. The name Cross Creek was assumed because the town was located at the juncture of two major waterways in the area.

A postcard depiction of John Newberry's old gristmill on Cross Creek. *Courtesy of Larry Tew.*

Merchants Richard Lyon and Hugh Fullerton built a trading post on Newberry's land. This particular mercantile business linked Cross Creek in the trading route of the Moravians in the north, the Piedmont in the west and the port of Wilmington in the south.

Cross Creek grew to be the second-largest settlement on the Cape Fear River. Because of its success, in 1761 the village of Cross Creek petitioned the state assembly to be incorporated into a town. Surprisingly, the assembly found Cross Creek to be an unsuitable town and instead ordered one hundred mostly swampy acres on the west bank of the Cape Fear to be surveyed for a town site to be called Campbellton.

Campbellton (sometimes also referenced as Cambelton, Cambellton and Campbeltown) was incorporated in 1762 in an area just south of Cross Creek and was named for a Mr. Farquard (sometimes also spelled Farquhard) Campbell. This honor was bestowed on Campbell because of his tireless work at developing the town and for doing so much in order to build it up, like petitioning for major buildings. The courthouse and jail were relocated there, making Campbellton the new county seat. Cross Creek residents did not like the new location at all and petitioned to have those public buildings moved again to drier land. They were only partially successful; the jail was moved.

Cape Fear River scenes adorn this postcard from the 1890s. *Courtesy of the North Carolina State Archives.*

This early sketch depicts the Town House in Campbellton, the heart of the city center. *Courtesy of the North Carolina State Archives.*

In 1765, another Quaker from Pennsylvania named Robert Cochran arrived at Campbellton. His intention was to build a mill, so he began surveying the waters of Blount and Cross Creeks. He found a suitable stretch on Cross Creek and built the first flouring mill in the eastern part of the state. When the mill was finished, a store was built adjacent to it. The store was kept well stocked. Wheat-laden wagons began coming in from the mountains and backcountry to trade. Business boomed for many years, especially as streets were established and other stores began opening. Flour production became so great that the excesses were shipped to the West Indies and other ports.

Rockfish Village was established in 1766. Located seven miles southwest of Campbellton, the Rockfish Manufacturing Company built the Little Rockfish Factory on Little Rockfish Creek. A fast current and abundance of trees led to the addition of lumber camps, a sawmill and a gristmill. Together with Campbellton and Cross Creek, the three areas worked together as trading centers, heading up navigation of the Cape Fear River with the major seaport in Wilmington.

The effect of such success in commerce caused an influx of people. The state's population was 250,000, with 5,000 people in the Campbellton and Cross Creek regions, making North Carolina the fourth most populous British colony.

As the colonies grew in size, dissatisfaction with the Crown of Great Britain also grew. Colonists began to fight for independence.

THE AMERICAN REVOLUTIONARY WAR

The era of the American Revolution was one of divided loyalties among Cumberland County's citizens. A number of people were staunchly devoted to the British Crown (these numbers came mostly from the Highland Scots). Those in opposition to the Crown were looking for a life independent from Europe. The county was heavily populated with active Patriots.

This circa 1935 photo depicts Liberty Point, where fifty-five Fayetteville men gathered to draft and sign the Liberty Point Resolves in 1775. *Library of Congress Prints & Photographs Division.*

On June 30, 1775, a rally at Cross Creek produced a document called the Cumberland Association but most widely known as the Liberty Point Resolves. A group of fifty-five men met at a tavern to sign this document protesting the actions of the British Crown following the Battles of Lexington and Concord.

Now, this document is unlike the Declaration of Independence in that it expresses hope that Great Britain and the colonies could reconcile their differences. Despite this earnest hope, the creators realized this was not a likely scenario. They vowed to "go forth and be ready to sacrifice our lives and fortunes to secure her [their new country's] freedom and safety."

The brief document read:

> *At a general meeting of the several Committees of the District of Wilmington, held at the Court-House in Wilmington, Tuesday, the 20th day of June, 1775:*
>
> *Resolved, That the following Association stand as the Association of this Committee, and that it be recommended to the inhabitants of this District to sign the same as speedily as possible.*
>
> *THE ASSOCIATION.*
>
> *The actual commencement of hostilities against the Continent by the British Troops, in the bloody scene on the nineteenth of April last, near Boston; the increase of arbitrary impositions, from a wicked and despotick Ministry; and the dread of instigated insurrection in the Colonies, are caused sufficient to drive an oppressed People to the use of arms: We, therefore, the subscribers of Cumberland County, holding ourselves bound by that most sacred of all obligations, the duty of good citizens towards an injured Country, and thoroughly convinced that under our distressed circumstances we shall be justified before you in resisting force by force; do unite ourselves under every tie of religion and honour, and associate as a band in her defence [sic] against every foe; hereby solemnly engaging, that whenever our Continental or Provincial Councils shall decree it necessary, we will go forth and be ready to sacrifice our lives and fortunes to secure her freedom and safety. This obligation to continue in full force until, a reconciliation shall take place between Great Britain and America, upon constitutional principles, an event we most ardently desire. And we will hold all those persons inimical to the liberty of the Colonies who shall refuse to subscribe to this Association; and we will in all things follow*

the advice of our General Committee, respecting the purposes aforesaid, the preservation of peace and good order, and the safety of individual and private property.

Colonel Robert Rowan signed first. Several long-standing Fayetteville names followed, most notably Gillespie, Barge, Carver, Green, Council, Elwell and Hollingsworth.

The Liberty Point Resolves were one of the earliest versions of a written pledge to obtain freedom from Great Britain and preceded the Declaration of Independence by more than a year.

THE WAR FINDS CUMBERLAND COUNTY

During the War for Independence, the opposing sides in North Carolina, and consequently Cross Creek, assumed the names of the English parliamentary parties. The Whigs were the Patriots in favor of independence, and the Tories were Loyalists to England.

In 1777, a test oath was deemed essential by the North Carolina General Assembly in order to truly determine those who were faithful to the Crown. All citizens were presented with an oath of fidelity to the state; those who refused it were required to give bond and leave the country within sixty days. There was a surprising number of Loyalists in the area, and they promptly began measures to leave the state. Some say as many as two-thirds of Cumberland County left the area.

The Highland Scots who remained loyal to King George left the Cape Fear country for Nova Scotia. It was an exodus akin to the one that occurred when they left Scotland after the Battle of Culloden, especially after the state refused to yield its position. The Highlanders settled in Nova Scotia under the British flag. Many families in that part of Canada trace their ancestry back to the Cape Fear Valley.

However, there must have been a loophole in the oath or a group of people who were not honest, because even after losing a great number, a large population of Loyalists still remained in Cumberland County.

During the war, the county mainly served as a granary and supply arsenal for military troops. Oftentimes, the city was filled with rumors of impending invasions. Despite these rumors, the city only saw actual battle twice: once in early 1776 and again in 1781 (the last year of the war). Between those two instances, there were plenty of skirmishes, although they mainly occurred between disgruntled local Whigs and Tories.

Cumberland County and Cross Creek's most influential contribution to the Revolutionary War happened in its earliest months, through participation in the Battle of Moore's Creek Bridge (North Carolina's first military action of the Revolutionary War). During this battle, which took place on February 26, 1776, a small Patriot army defeated a group of Highland Scots marching toward Wilmington from Cross Creek. The royal governor had summoned the Highland Scots, who then went and rallied for soldiers at Cross Hill (later to be called Carthage), followed by Cross Creek, in order to please the royal governor with their numbers. There is a legend that this group of Highland Scots was spurred on by the famous Flora MacDonald.

FLORA MACDONALD

Flora MacDonald is a heroine of rebel Scottish legend. She rescued Bonnie Prince Charlie from local militia during the Jacobite uprising during the Battle of Culloden in Scotland. The commander of the local militia was her stepfather, Hugh MacDonald, who gave her a pass to leave their island home of Benbecula. Included in the pass was clearance for a "manservant," whom Flora called "Betty Burke." The prince was disguised as Betty Burke. They fled the island on June 27, 1746.

Eventually captured, Flora was arrested and brought to London for aiding the prince's escape. She was imprisoned for a short spell in the Tower of London. She was allowed to live outside of the tower as long as she worked under the guard of a "messenger." She was released in 1747 after the passing of the Act of Indemnity.

Shortly thereafter, Flora married Allan MacDonald of Kingsburgh. They had five sons and two daughters. In 1774, the family immigrated to North Carolina. During the Revolution, her husband, then Captain MacDonald, served the British government in the Eighty-fourth Regiment of Foot.

On February 18, 1776, the Highland Army was preparing to march out of Cross Creek toward Wilmington. Flora MacDonald mounted a white horse, rode up and down the rows of soldiers and rallied them in what is said

Flora MacDonald (1722–1790) is most well known for saving Prince Charlie from falling into the hands of his enemies. *Courtesy of Larry Tew.*

to have been a cheery and animated manner. She and her horse stood under an oak tree and surveyed the troops. It is believed that this tree still stands on Cool Springs Street.

Her spirited attempts at rousing the troops were successful, and they marched along beating drums, flying flags, playing pipes and sharing spirited songs and stories of Scotland. Despite their high energy, the Loyalists were defeated at the Battle of Moore's Creek Bridge.

During the battle, Flora's husband was captured and held prisoner for two years until a prisoner exchange occurred in 1777. At that time, he was sent to Fort Edward, Nova Scotia, to continue his command of the Eighty-fourth Regiment of Foot. During the years of her husband's imprisonment, Flora was in hiding herself. American Patriots ravaged her plantation in Cross Creek, taking everything she owned. After her husband's release, Flora joined him in Fort Edward. In 1779, Flora and her daughter Fanny returned to Scotland to live with her other daughter, Anne. When the war ended, Allan also returned and regained possession of the family estate in Kingsburgh. They lived out their days in Scotland. And so Cross Creek's brief hold on Flora MacDonald ended.

A Story of the Revolution

Legend has it that during the Revolutionary War, a German tailor lived near the Market House. He rented a room above a store in Market Square where he lived and worked. The tailor lived and breathed by the American way. Though his accent was thick, his devotion to North Carolina was thicker. When a company of British troops camping near Fayetteville caught wind of his apparent disloyalty to King George, it decided to raid his home.

When the soldiers arrived at his home, they began roughing up the poor tailor. Upon finding an empty wooden barrel at the top of the stairs, they shoved him in headfirst and threw the barrel down the stairway. When the barrel hit the pavement, they say the "fat little tailor popped out of the barrel, struggled to his feet" and exclaimed in his thick accent, "True Whig to the last by God! True Whig to the last!"

Cornwallis

The largest armed conflict in the Southern Campaign took place in the late summer of 1781 at the Guilford County Courthouse in present-day Greensboro (about one hundred miles northwest of Fayetteville). British Lieutenant General Lord Charles Cornwallis led the battle, and though he won, the victory cost him over 25 percent of his army. After the battle, Cornwallis turned toward Wilmington. He stopped in Cross Creek for a few days in the hopes of resting his troops.

He expected to find food and Loyalist support, none of which was readily offered. He did not stay in town long. During his brief stay, Cornwallis happened upon a plantation and was surprisingly cordial. The account can be found in Cornelia Phillips Spencer's book *The Last Ninety Days of the War in North Carolina* and reads:

When Lord Cornwallis was on his march to Wilmington, after the battle of Guilford Court-House, passing by the residence of a planter near Cross Creek, the army halted. The young mistress of the mansion, a gay and very beautiful matron of eighteen, with the impulsive curiosity of a child, ran to her front piazza to gaze at the pageant. Some officers dismounting approached the house. She addressed one of the foremost, and begged that he would point out to her Lord Cornwallis, if he were there, for "she wished to see a Lord." "Madam," said the gentleman, removing his hat, "I am Lord Cornwallis." Then with the formal courtesy of the day he led her into the house, giving to the frightened family every assurance of protection. With the high breeding of a gentleman and the frankness of a soldier, he won all hearts during his stay, from the venerable grandmother in her chair to the gay girl who had first accosted him. While the army remained, not an article was disturbed on the plantation, though, as he himself warned them, there were stragglers in his wake whom he could not detect, and who failed not to do what mischief they could in the way of plundering, after he had passed.

Cornwallis's warning was not just for show. British soldiers came into town and caused a terrible amount of destruction. The grandson of the "gay and beautiful matron," Charles B. Mallet, also gave an account of the great army passing over the same land (the two accounts are vastly different and beg explanation that will probably never be given):

The china and glass-ware were all carried out of the house by the soldiers, and deliberately smashed in the yard. The furniture—piano, beds, tables, bureaus—were all cut to pieces with axes; the pantries and smoke-houses were stripped of their contents; the houses were all plundered; the poultry, cows, horses, etc., were shot down and carried off; and then, after all this, the houses were all fired and burned to the ground.

Whether or not he pillaged, Cornwallis's true reason for coming to Cross Creek was to replenish his arms and armies. The Highland Scots of the area maintained loyalty to the British Crown and began following Cornwallis at the beginning of the war. Large numbers of Scots were lost at the Battle of Guilford Courthouse, so Cornwallis decided, when coming through Cross

Creek (as the unofficial headquarters of the Highland Scots), that he would attempt to rebuild his numbers.

The Highland Scots met him with great kindness and offered fifteen hundred men, but with the stipulation that their own officials would command them. Despite the fact that Cornwallis desperately needed the bodies, he refused. No compromise could be found, so Cornwallis left town without any additional soldiers, arms or food. His course of action changed, and instead of marching to Wilmington, he turned to Virginia, only to surrender at Yorktown in October.

If Cornwallis had come to a compromise with those fifteen hundred Highland Scots and they had continued to Wilmington to form a new army with the British regulars there and stock up on arms, the outcome of the Revolutionary War may have been different. Surrender at Yorktown may have never occurred. The life and history of North Carolina, and the United States, might have been different if the Highland Scots of Cross Creek hadn't said no to Cornwallis.

Cornwallis's surrender at Yorktown, however, did not mark the complete end of the Revolutionary War. The Whigs and Tories remained embroiled in their bitter war for another year. On August 14, 1781, a group of Tories led by David Fanning descended on Cross Creek and, with their army of six hundred men, forcibly took control of the town. They immediately began taking prisoners. They captured fifty Patriots, including famous colonels Emmett and Rowan, as well as a few prominent citizens (like Robert Cochran, the second Quaker settler), among others. Skirmishes and battles continued for months, continuing to wreak havoc on the land and economy of the Cross Creek area. Many soldiers were left with nothing.

Finally, the stormy clouds of the Revolution passed on. Savannah, Georgia, and Charleston, South Carolina (two heavily occupied cities), were evacuated of British troops in the last months of 1782. In Versailles, France, in November 1782, the independence of the United States was acknowledged in a provisional treaty. The final peace treaty was signed in Paris in September 1783. The last of the British troops left American soil on November 25, 1783. The Revolutionary War and all of its extraneous battles were finally, finally over.

As John Oates wrote in his book *The Story of Fayetteville*, "Let us not forget that the patriots of the Cape Fear began early, fought long and never stopped until the last bugle for battle was sounded and the last of the enemies of freedom driven out."

II
FAYETTEVILLE'S
GOLDEN AGE

Life after the Revolutionary War was able to continue on in a relatively normal way. Business owners and shopkeepers were able to resume work, while the soldiers who were left with nothing slowly began to rebuild their lives. The areas of Campbellton and Cross Creek continued to draw both trade and settlers. Eventually, the idea of a merger was voiced.

THE ERA OF FAYETTEVILLE

In 1778, Campbellton and Cross Creek were merged into one town under the name Upper Campbellton (from Cross Creek) and Lower Campbellton (from Campbellton). The idea behind the merger was that the two settlements were in such proximity that it would be beneficial to work as one entity in trading affairs (mostly because Cross Creek was still an unincorporated village while Campbellton was a town proper). Moreover, the General Assembly's initial intention was that Campbellton would be the center of trade; however, its location on the Cape Fear River was in a swampy area, and it lacked the services of Cross Creek. Citizens knew this and promptly drew up a petition to highlight Cross Creek's advantages in order to have business centered on their town.

The petition seems to have been drawn up in 1780 and read:

> *To the Honorable General Assembly of the State of North Carolina, The Petition of the freeholders and inhabitants of the County of Cumberland,* Humbly Sheweth *That the village called Cross Creek, within the Liberties of Campbellton, has within a few years increased in a rapid manner, insomuch that there are one hundred dwelling houses and Merchants' Stores therein, and the Trade of the back settlements (before the beginning of the present wars), almost wholly centering there, occasioned originally by the convenience of the Flour Mills on Cross Creek, of which there are now Three, and the best in this State; That the situation of Cross Creek is High, dry and healthy, and accommodated with excellent Water, & that of Campbellton, as laid out by act of Assembly, is mostly in a low, swampy situation, & the road from Cross Creek thereto is through a level clay ground, which from the constant intercourse of Waggons, is often rendered almost impassable for foot persons and extremely disagreeable to horse-men; That, as business is transacted entirely at Cross Creek, and the inhabitants of the County generally make their Markets in Term time, it is extremely difficult to enforce the attendance of witnesses and Jurors at a Mile distance, by reason of which the business of the Court is greatly retarded; That, to avoid all invidious disturbances for the future, and to regulate the Village of Cross Creek by a Law for that purpose, Commissioners be appointed to lay out the streets thereof with as much convenience and as little damage to the inhabitants & owners of houses & land as may be; and that for the future the said Village and Town be distinguished by the names of Upper and Lower Campbellton; That for several years past the County has been without a Gaol* [traditional spelling of jail]*, and the Court house being at present in a very ruinous condition, that an act be passed for building a new Court House & Gaol, in the upper Town, now called Cross Creek, and that the Courts be held in such Court House, when built…That Your Petitioners therefore Pray the Premises may be taken into consideration, and that your Petitioners may have such relief as to Equity and Justice may seem meet; and your Petitioners, as in duty bound, shall Pray.*

The petition was signed by at least ninety men, most notably Robert Rowan (the first signee and probably the drafter), John Dobbins, William Carver and Robert Cochran.

Their petition was somewhat successful. Trade centered on Robert Cochran's Mill in Cross Creek, though they received little funding for building revitalization. Citizens complained that Campbellton received funding for improvements when Cross Creek needed them more because it had more to offer. Even so, the two towns did indeed merge, with the intention of being called Upper and Lower Campbellton.

The two incorporated towns were still mostly referred to as Cross Creek out of sheer habit (or plain stubbornness); the name of Campbellton seemed to just fall away. Cross Creek continued to grow. Then, in 1783, an act was proposed by the General Assembly to establish a permanent state capital. Realizing that Cross Creek had been virtually untouched by the Revolutionary War, considering the fact that the North Carolina General Assembly already convened in Cross Creek and taking into account that it was already a major hub of commerce, trade and political activity, the city was named as a candidate (as were the other North Carolina cities of Tarboro and Hillsborough).

Cross Creek was spruced up: a plan of streets and a town square was laid out in a gridlike pattern. The blueprints were typical of eighteenth-century designs for towns. Additionally, the 1783 act changed the name of the town yet again. The new name would be Fayetteville, one of the first of many cities in the United States to be named for the Revolutionary War hero the Marquis de Lafayette.

In 1788, a Wilmington journalist published an article in an attempt to bolster Fayetteville's favor as state capital. The article depicted Fayetteville in a lovely light:

> *A traveler who has lately traveled through this state, informs us, that he has no where observed so much public spirit, as in Fayette-Ville. At that place they have lately opened several new roads, and raised a number of new bridges, in order to render the communication with the country more easy and convenient. They have also erected two large and elegant buildings for the accommodation of their courts and General Assembly.*
>
> *There is a company formed to make Cross-Creek navigable for boats from the river to the upper town.*
>
> *All these improvements are carried out by private subscriptions.*
>
> *This proposed navigation of the Creek, will, as expected, greatly lessen the expense which is occasioned by conveying merchandize* [sic] *and etc.*

from the landing to the town in wagons as well as add much to the beauty of the place.

In short, it is the opinion of our correspondent, that, considering the situation of Fayette-Ville, so convenient for commanding the trade of an extensive back country, and its other advantages, that it must soon become a place of great consequence, as well as worthy of being the Capital of an extensive state.

Despite all these positive changes, Fayetteville lost out on the state capital bid by a single vote. The holdout came from one Timothy Bloodworth of New Hanover County; after the vote, he was promptly elected to the United States Senate, with little explanation. The subject is still sorely debated around town, as true Fayetteville natives still feel there may have been some foul play or bribery surrounding Bloodworth.

Instead of Fayetteville, a spot of land on Joel Lane's plantation in Wake County was picked, on the grounds that it was closer to the center of the state than Fayetteville. Despite the fact that there was no existing town in Wake County, a popular tavern was located there. It is said that many legislative officials preferred to convene at the bar, so Raleigh won out as capital. There is one theory about how Mr. Lane's land was chosen.

On the night the commissioners met to pick a precise spot for the capitol building, the tavern's owner was selling large servings of a popular drink called cherry bounce. Perhaps the commissioners all had a bit too much to drink because the next day they found they had agreed to buy one thousand acres of fellow commissioner Joel Lane's land and accepted his proposal to build the town there (despite the fact that it was ten whole miles from the tavern they all so favored). No details on the agreement were made; there was no record explaining their decision and no minutes detailing the meeting.

Fayetteville natives were frustrated because their city was already waiting and willing. There was no need to spend more time and money waiting for an entire city and state building to be erected. Townsfolk drew up a petition that was passed around town, stating, "The establishment of a seat of government in a place unconnected with commerce and where there is at present no town would be a heavy expense to the people" and that "the town when established never can rise above the degree of a village." But alas, their petition didn't change anything. The legislature continued to meet in Fayetteville until the new capitol building was built in Raleigh in 1792.

ALL THE NEWS THAT'S FIT TO PRINT

The year 1789 was an especially noteworthy one for the town. North Carolina's first printing press was built, and the *North Carolina Chronicle & Fayetteville Gazette* became the city's first newspaper. John Sibley, a politically active physician in town, founded the paper. The paper was housed at the print shop on Green Street, often referred to as "under Franklin's head" because the shop was under a sign in the shape of a silhouette of Benjamin Franklin.

During the newspaper's first year, it was able to announce that the first United States senator, Samuel Johnson, was voted in during a General Assembly session at Fayetteville's statehouse. Johnson then voted to cede North Carolina's western land for what would become the state of Tennessee.

A September 21, 1789 edition of the *Fayetteville Gazette* contained an advertisement for the opening of a new tavern in town, the Cool Springs Tavern. The advertisement read:

Cool Springs Tavern, built in the late 1700s, is one of (if not *the*) oldest buildings still standing in Fayetteville. *Courtesy of the North Carolina State Archives.*

The subscriber begs leave to inform the public that he has opened a Public House in Fayetteville—near the Cool Spring. Every exertion will be made to oblige those who may please to favor him with their custom. Sept. 14, 1789. Dolphin Davis.

Cool Springs was a major water source for the town until the early twentieth century. An old folk legend says that anyone who drinks from Cool Springs will someday return to Fayetteville. The tavern was built right next to the springs and managed to survive the centuries' worth of calamities that befell the city (everything from fire to flood to termites). It still stands today as one of the oldest structures in Fayetteville.

The newspaper also broke the news that the legislature chartered the University of North Carolina (UNC) to be built at New Hope Chapel Hill just outside of Raleigh. UNC–Chapel Hill is America's first and oldest state university. To wrap up such a newsworthy year, on November 21, 1789, the General Assembly met in Fayetteville and voted to accept the United States Constitution, making North Carolina the twelfth state to enter the federal Union. Delegates of the state convention were housed at Cool Springs Tavern.

THE FAYETTEVILLE INDEPENDENT LIGHT INFANTRY

On March 5, 1792, under President George Washington's administration, Congress passed the Militia Act, a decree to form state-operated militia comprising men ages eighteen to forty-five. With the talk of war with England, Fayetteville organized the Fayetteville Independent Light Infantry (FILI) on August 23, 1793. Each militia company was authorized one captain, one lieutenant and one ensign.

The FILI, a "corps of gentlemen," elected Robert Adam as captain, John Winslow as lieutenant and Robert Cochran as ensign. The original 1793 charter muster roll contained the following guardsmen (including several names still prominent in town): Isham Blake, Andrew Broadfoot, John Eccles, A. Ferguson, Sam Goodwin, Jacob Hartman, Dillon Jordan, John Lumsden, Thomas Matthews, Kennith Murchison, Hugh McDonald, James McIntyre, William McLean McKay, Hugh McLean, John McLeod, John McMillan, A. McQueen, Silver Selan Selbane, George Thompson and John Thompson.

At the FILI's inception, war threatened almost all the European powers, and with Spain's hostile attitude toward the United States, the South again braced for war. The FILI made itself available. In 1797, war threatened to erupt between France and the United States. Again, the FILI was ready. Its services were finally called upon during the War of 1812.

During the war, North Carolina's main military concern was to protect its coastline. British warships kept an almost constant presence off the coast, and there was always fear of British attack. On July 11, 1813, a British fleet containing one large battleship and several hundred smaller boats landed at Ocracoke on the northern coast of North Carolina. Adjutant General Calvin Jones sent a call to action, saying, "Our State has been invaded, and this is the moment of my departure for New Bern. All those who may tender their services are invited immediately to repair to New Bern, armed efficiently with muskets, rifles, sabers and pistols, to be organized under my order."

In preparation of their departure, a meeting of the FILI members took place on July 19, 1813. Minutes of the meeting were kept:

At a meeting of the Fayetteville Independent Light Infantry Company held at the Town House this day, for the purpose of making necessary arrangement, preparatory to their departure from this place, agreeable to the order of Brigadier General (Thomas) Davis, for the defense of the sea coast, the following resolutions were approved, viz. Resolved that Duncan Thompson and John Huske be appointed to provide bread, bacon and spirits, for the general use of the Company. Resolved that John Smith and John R. Adam be a committee for the purpose of providing wagons, pots, kettles and all other things necessary for the use of the Company. Resolved that the sum of five dollars be collected from each member of the Company for the purchase of the above articles, and paid to the above committees. Resolved that the Company meet tomorrow morning, wearing uniforms for the purpose of having their arms examined.

The Fayetteville Arsenal was ordered to be cleared of munitions and taken by the FILI to the defense of Wilmington. The FILI was in full service in Wilmington until its service was discharged.

The Fayetteville Independent Light Infantry remains the oldest military unit in North Carolina and the second-oldest militia unit in the United

States. During its years of service as a military company, it has been actively engaged twice. Today, the FILI is still an active ceremonial unit and is North Carolina's official historic military command. William Barry Grove coined the FILI's motto at its organization, "He that hath no stomach to this fight, let him depart." It lives by that motto still.

EDUCATION

Early settlers to Fayetteville came with an abiding appreciation of freedom, religion and, most importantly, education. A school opened in 1794 and was incorporated as the Fayetteville Academy for Males and Females in 1799.

In 1825, Raleigh's newspaper, the *Raleigh Register*, published an article citing the Fayetteville Academy as a most prestegious institution, offering room and board for all scholars. The article went on to say:

> *The Academy lot and building are situated in a very pleasant part of the town, on one of the principal streets and in the neighborhood of the Episcopal and Presbyterian churches. The lot is large and well shaded, in the front yard, which communicates with the street over a stile. The main building and wing are three stories high with a double portico in front, and is surmounted with a beautiful belfry.*

Several men of note graduated from the Fayetteville Academy. Among them were William Rufus King (eventual vice president of the United States); John Owen (governor of North Carolina in 1828); John Eccles (distinguished Fayetteville lawyer); Warren Winslow (member of Congress and governor of North Carolina); and Judah P. Benjamin (senator from Louisiana and secretary of state in the cabinet of Confederate president Jefferson Davis).

During the 1800s, it was not uncommon for local preachers to be the most prominent schoolteachers in towns. Reverend David Kerr was the first Presbyterian minister in Fayetteville, and he was also the first principal of the academy.

Another major educational institution of note was the Donaldson Academy and Labor School, opened in 1832.

Fayetteville trade route grew so large that at one time a large part of eastern Tennessee, southwestern Virginia and all of the immediate counties surrounding Cumberland looked to Fayetteville for supplies of salt, iron and other merchandise. Despite its average size, Fayetteville was easily one of the most important places.

Judah P. Benjamin attended school in Fayetteville and went on to become a senator in Louisiana. *Library of Congress Prints & Photographs Division.*

The Donaldson School soon became quite the rival of the Fayetteville Academy. Its charges even began to increase in order to be considered akin to the academy. In December 1833, the school adopted the following schedule of fees:

That the price of board at Steward's Hall for table expenses—$5.00 per month; washing .50 cents per month; lodging .50 cents per month; room rent .50 cents per month. Room furnishings (other than bedding, fire wood, and candles) to be furnished by the students.

The Donaldson Academy continued to thrive until 1883, when the property was leased to the Graded School Trustees.

In the late 1830s, another institution, called the Fayetteville Female Seminary, was opened in Fayetteville. It advertised in 1839 that it had eighty-four students who learned all the following subjects: Latin, French, arithmetic, geometry, English grammar, geography, intellectual philosophy, chemistry, astronomy, reading, writing and spelling. Essentially, what was deemed the "fundamentals" of schools of the day. Its term ran from the fourteenth of October to the eighteenth of July, divided into two semesters lasting twenty weeks each. The charge was eight dollars per semester.

GOLD

Gold was one of the most sought-after resources of the New World, and the Fayetteville area was not spared seekers. In 1799, a fairly significant amount of gold was found by a young man named Conrad Reed. He and his younger siblings were fishing in a Cabarrus County creek when he found a shiny, seventeen-pound "rock."

Not knowing its importance, the rock was used as a doorstop for upwards of three years. Eventually, Conrad's father, John, took the rock to the closest jeweler—a Fayetteville man. The jeweler melted the rock down to a bar that measured about six inches long. Sources provide conflicting descriptions of the jeweler. Some describe him as somewhat of a scam artist who used Reed's naiveté to his advantage, offering a selling price of just $3.50. Other historical accounts say that Reed is the one who offered the price of $3.50, thinking that was a decent asking price, and the jeweler simply didn't correct him. Regardless of whether the jeweler was an upstanding citizen, Reed didn't really know the value of the gold, and he received only $3.50 for it. In actuality, it was worth $3,600.00.

It didn't take long for Reed to learn the error of his ways. He later sued the jeweler and was supposedly awarded the sum of about $1,000.

Because of his literal good fortune, Reed soon began searching for more and more stones. During the next year, he found "nuggets" weighing up to twenty-eight pounds. News of his finds spread quickly, and soon the Sandhill area of North Carolina was overtaken by prospectors. New mines were reported every week and sometimes almost daily.

In fact, the state was so prosperous that a mint in Charlotte was opened in 1837. Most of the area's larger quantities were taken to Charlotte to be coined until 1861, when the Confederate government appropriated the mint. Just in that time span alone, however, the mint coined over $4.5 million in North Carolina gold (a definite portion of which came from the Fayetteville area of the state).

The discovery of gold brought scores of new people to the area and, consequently, new pocketbooks. Fayetteville and Cumberland County prospered under the emergence of industries like wagon making, gristmills, nail factories, tobacco factories and other textiles. And so, at the turn of the century in 1800, Fayetteville saw somewhat of an industrial revolution.

Fayetteville's trade route grew so large that at one time a large part of eastern Tennessee, southwestern Virginia and all of the immediate counties surrounding Cumberland looked to Fayetteville for supplies of salt, iron and other merchandise. Despite its average size, Fayetteville was easily one of the state's most important places.

THE FAYETTEVILLE POSTAL SERVICE

One of the first post offices established in North Carolina was built in Fayetteville in 1798. The post office was part of the original "mail post road," a 1,765-mile post line running from Schoodic, Maine, to St. Mary's, Georgia. At the time, North Carolina had few other post offices. Fayetteville was connected to Warrenton, Louisburg, Raleigh, Averasboro

The post office was the first federally financed building in Fayetteville since the U.S. Arsenal. It was completed in 1910. *Courtesy of Larry Tew.*

and Lumberton through the mail post road. Fayetteville had its own line to Wilmington that totaled 118 miles.

There seems to be no existing record of where the first post office building (or buildings, for that matter) was located. A federal building to house the post office didn't open until 1910. This was the first federally financed building to be built in Fayetteville since the United States Arsenal before the Civil War. Until then, the post office would move from place to place and would often be located in the corner of a store.

These stores became quite popular and profited from housing the post office. Because there were only weekly (no daily) newspapers, the postmaster acted as a sort of dispenser of information. News, by word of mouth, came from him, so these stores became great gathering places.

TRANSPORTATION

As trade expanded and Fayetteville grew as an economic center, there was a great need to improve land and water transportation. There were few designated roads in the state, and even then, their condition was rough. With rail transportation still years away, the main dependence continued to be on water transportation.

In 1817, Captain Otway Burns of Beaufort began work on a steamboat he would call *Prometheus*. It was a stern-wheel vessel that sailed the Cape Fear River transporting goods between Wilmington, Fayetteville and Smithville (also called Southport). The next year, a second steamboat was introduced.

James Sewell built the *Henrietta* in 1818 on his plantation on the east side of the Cape Fear River; his homestead was three miles north of Campbellton. Named for Sewell's daughter, the steamer first sailed the Cape Fear River on April 30, 1818, under the command of Captain Charles Taws. In early July 1818, the steamer made its first trip from Fayetteville to Wilmington. Because water was low, the distance of 115 miles took six days. The maximum speed reached by the boat was 8 miles an hour.

Mechanical problems caused the *Henrietta* a lot of early troubles, and it was very difficult to steer. In order for the steamboat to manage sharp turns, oftentimes crew members had to secure a rope around a tree or rock on the shore and pull the boat around. A captain out of Philadelphia got hold of the *Henrietta* in 1820 and changed the vessel's gearing to a chain-motion drive. With the improvements in maneuverability, and with its new commander, Captain Benjamin Rush, the *Henrietta* was able to increase its passenger and freight services.

The *Henrietta* sailed the Cape Fear River until 1865, when one of the boilers aboard the steamer exploded, sinking the boat immediately. At that time, the *Henrietta* was the oldest steamboat in the United States. Over the next few years, a few of the boilers were retrieved from the water and sold for farm use. Parts were still being recovered in June 1891, when it was said that "the bones" of the *Henrietta* were "still visible and rotting below the city." It was suggested that the wreck be preserved as a historic relic.

FAYETTEVILLE & WESTERN

In 1846, plans were made to improve the road situation in the state. Dr. Elisha Mitchell was hired to route a turnpike connecting Raleigh and Fayetteville with the western portions of the state. Even though the plan was simply to have dirt roads, they would be a great improvement over what existed.

For the Fayetteville portion of the road, two potential routes were mapped out. One went through Troy in Montgomery County, and one passed through Carthage and Asheboro to the northwest. To Mitchell, neither seemed viable, as he found the Sandhills extremely difficult to navigate. He wrote in a commentary:

> *Through the greater part of 30 miles after we strike the sand, there is no road, but every person selects a route for himself, following the general course of previous travel along the ridge that separates the waters which flow into the Cape Fear, from those that run into the two PeeDees. It is in fact the old trail by which Buffaloes and Indians used to come down from the interior to the coast. One is often uncertain, whilst attempting to follow it, whether he is advancing towards the end of his journey, or merely crossing diagonally from one side of the ridge to the other.*

The turnpikes were never constructed because the project never received financial backing from Fayetteville residents and business leaders, most of whom were interested in pushing railroad travel. Dr. Mitchell was expressly against rail travel. And so it seemed that the main advocates for bettering statewide transportation were at an impasse.

Thankfully, the advent of plank roads came about. Used widely in the forests of Russia and Canada, plank roads were built of wood and were developed to provide a reliable road surface across difficult terrain. They were less expensive than railroads and easier to follow than dirt paths. There finally seemed to be an answer for those stuck in a deadlock.

In January 1849, the Fayetteville & Western Plank Road Company was chartered to begin construction. Because construction officials and engineers had never built a plank road before, work was slow. It took more than a year to complete a 12.8-mile section of road. The design for a plank road was very specific, calling for it to be eight feet wide. First, land was graded for good drainage from rainfall, and then four timbers (also called "stringers") were laid lengthwise and connected by thick five- by eight-foot planks. Every third plank was cut four inches shorter with the idea that it would allow vehicles easy access back onto the road should they have to pull off.

The final step in the construction was to coat the road with a layer of fine sand. The theory for this action was that the small grains of sand would penetrate the wood grain, seep into the cracks and fibers and mix with any droppings on the road to create a hard, tough covering. The covering would be something like felt and would protect the wood from wheels and horses' hooves.

That first section of road opened in April 1850. Small sections were completed connecting cities all over the state. By 1854, Fayetteville was connected to Carthage, Salem, Salisbury and Bethania, just to name a few. The total length of the Fayetteville & Western Plank Road was 129 miles. To this day, it stands as the longest wooden highway ever constructed.

Even with this distinction, the Fayetteville & Western Plank Road Company failed to plan for the major expense of maintaining the road (which was especially prone to cracked planks and holes that were dangerous for horses). The company tried many ways to cheaply improve the road, but nothing worked. Because the road conditions were poor, fewer people traveled them. Consequently, fewer toll fees were collected, so there was no money to repair the roads. Rail travel was being heavily pushed, with Fayetteville finally succumbing to the ease and reliability of iron tracks. The Fayetteville & Western Plank Road Company faded away.

The Fayetteville Observer

After the establishment of the *North Carolina Chronicle & Fayetteville Gazette*, six other weekly publications were started. All of them were short-lived. Then, in 1816, Francis W. Waldo launched the *Carolina Observer*. In 1835, the newspaper would finally change its name permanently to the *Fayetteville Observer*.

Edward J. Hale assumed ownership of the newspaper in 1825. Hale was a printer and writer for newspapers in Raleigh and Washington before coming to Fayetteville, and he was an outspoken Whig supporter. The *Fayetteville Observer* became somewhat of a leading political journal and played a pivotal role in bringing telegraph lines to the city. Most major newspapers of the day were printing news they received via the wire, and never one to be left out, Fayetteville brought in telegraph lines in 1847.

Hale ran the paper until 1865, when, because of the newspaper's strong pro-Southern voice, Sherman's army destroyed the plant. After the war, Hale handed the reins to his sons, who resumed publishing in 1883. The Hale name remains a prominent one in Fayetteville to this day. The *Fayetteville Observer* holds the distinction of being North Carolina's oldest newspaper still being published.

Churches

Records indicate that in 1800, Fayetteville still did not have an established church. Congregations were organized, of course, but they did not yet convene in actual churches (for none had been built). The primary denominations of the day were Presbyterian, Baptist and Quaker. The oldest organized congregation was the Presbyterians of Old Bluff (comprising congregations from Bluff, Barbeque and Longstreet). This congregation began meeting in 1758; its church building was erected in the mid-1850s.

One of the most noteworthy religious men of Fayetteville was the Reverend Henry Evans. Evans was a freeborn black man from Virginia, becoming one of the state's first blacks to receive a preaching license. On a Charleston, South Carolina trek, Evans stopped in Fayetteville for a few days. A short biography of Henry Evans was completed by Joyce Codrington. She wrote that

This circa 1930s photo shows Old Bluff Church, home to the oldest organized religious congregation in Fayetteville. *Library of Congress Prints & Photographs Division.*

he observed that the people of his race were lewd and expressed themselves with a great deal of profanity. They had never heard preaching from any denomination. This unwholesome and unchristian condition caused Evans to stay in Fayetteville and minister to those of his race.

He was met with great success, prompting Evans to construct a small meetinghouse (the unofficial first church structure in Fayetteville). As he didn't have a boat, Evans swam back and forth across the Cape Fear River carrying lumber and other supplies to build his structure. Finished in 1776 on land he had leased for seven years, Evans began preaching to a crowd of both blacks and whites—something that was relatively unheard of. He was so successful that in 1789, Henry Evans was named the city's "Most Remarkable Man." People began attending in such great numbers that the First Methodist Church was officially chartered in 1801.

The biography of Henry Evans reveals much about his life in Fayetteville, both the good and bad:

The news spread quickly about the success of the church and it was not long before Evans met with opposition. His preaching aroused enthusiasm in those who heard him and the town council became alarmed. They felt it was dangerous to have a black preacher with the ability, influence and the effectiveness of Henry Evans in the community and therefore ordered Evans to stop preaching. Evans continued to preach, despite the council's orders, but sought out locations which were not known to the council. He held services secretly, in the sandhills and in the woods, constantly changing locations, and even broke ice to swim across the Cape Fear River to preach on the other side. In this manner he evaded the town council, but soon after was sought by a lynch mob, which he also evaded. Despite these obstacles, Evans continued to preach in Fayetteville, eventually converting slaves and their masters as well.

The town council eventually revoked its order.

Evans was known as the "Father of Methodism" in Fayetteville. He died in 1810 and was buried beneath his church's structure. A newspaper article states:

His funeral at the church was attended by a greater concourse of persons than had been seen on any funeral occasion before. The whole community appeared to mourn his death, and the universal feeling seemed to be that in honoring the memory of Henry Evans we were paying a tribute to virtue and religion.

When Evans's Metropolitan AME Zion Church on Cool Spring Street was constructed in 1893, members had his body moved and entombed beneath the chancel of the church.

Though Evan's meetinghouse was undoubtedly important, it is still not listed as the first official church structure in Fayetteville. The First Presbyterian Church holds that honor. First Presbyterian, which was organized in 1800, built a church in 1816. Structural plans had been in the work since 1809, but funds were desperately needed before construction could begin. The Reverend Colin McIver, stated clerk of the session, was appointed to travel the country soliciting funds. He made a northern excursion and collected $293. During the northern excursion, McIver received donations from several prominent men, including President James Monroe, who donated $25, and Secretary of State John Quincy Adams, who donated $10.

The first stone of construction was laid on April 21, 1816, and the building was used continuously for church services and local meetings for the next fifteen years. The original structure burned in 1831 but was rebuilt almost immediately on the old walls. Construction was said to be so dangerous (perhaps because of the sheer height of the church's roof and steeple) that prayer committees were formed to pray solely for construction workers and their safety. The new building was completed on August 12, 1832, and was dedicated the same day.

To this day, the original 1832 chandeliers still hang in the front vestibule. Because they burn whale oil, they are no longer used, but they are there all the same. Additionally, in 1824, the Society of Young Ladies presented a silver Communion service consisting of a breadbasket, two cups and a tankard. These silver pieces survived the fire of 1831 and are still used in every Communion service. When not in use, they are carefully preserved in the church's historical room.

The First Presbyterian Church's tall steeple has been part of the Fayetteville skyline since 1831. *Library of Congress Prints & Photographs Division.*

Easily one of the most historic sites in Fayetteville, First Presbyterian contains lots of stories, one of which stems from a 1940s joke. As Oates described:

> *In the 1940s, the First Presbyterian Church spire was struck twice by lightning. A member of another denomination was twitting Parker Vickery (a Presbyterian) about it and said to him, "The Lord must have something against you Presbyterians. Lightning has never struck our church." Vickery quickly replied, "The Lord doesn't even know that you have a church here." That ended the conversation.*

In addition to the protestant denominations, Fayetteville (forever determined to be noteworthy) also had a thriving and prominent Roman Catholic Church. This was unusual for the South, especially in the early 1800s. Irish immigrants John Kelly and the Jordan family are especially noted for bringing this Catholic influence to the area. Kelly was a local merchant; the elder Jordan was a tavern keeper and the younger was a lawyer. The Roman Catholic chapel was built in 1829 on Bow Street, kitty-corner to Liberty Point. Rebuilt after the fire of 1831, the congregation continued to meet at that location for more than one hundred years.

Liberty Point and the first Catholic church (1832) in North Carolina stand at the intersection of Bow and Person Streets. *Courtesy of Larry Tew.*

By 1850, it was evident that Fayetteville had become heavily influenced by religion. As Roy Parker wrote, Fayetteville had a "quickening of religious interest and denominational zeal in the antebellum years." This was evident in the 1850 Fayetteville census. It listed twelve Baptist, eight Methodist, five Presbyterian, five Episcopal and five Roman Catholic churches established in Cumberland County.

THE TOWN HOUSE/MARKETPLACE

In 1817, Fayetteville town commissioners passed an ordinance stating that the first Town House would be the town marketplace. The ordinance read:

> *Be it ordained: That the underpart of the Town House is established as the Market Place for said town. There shall be a clerk appointed for the Market whose duty it will be to see that the rules and regulations be duly observed; to keep the Market clear; to superintend the weights and measures; shall see that such articles as are exposed for sale in the Market are of good and wholesome quality, etc., etc.*

The market opened at 7:00 a.m. and, on a typical day, saw merchants selling things like fresh pork, mutton, venison, poultry, cheese, butter, eggs, vegetables, hog's lard, fruits, corn and oats (among so many other wares). Butchers were able to lease individual stalls, and for years, sale continued under the Town House's iconic arches.

Merchants traveled great distances (some almost two hundred miles) for the privilege to sell at the Fayetteville marketplace. The trip would sometimes take days. On almost any night in the fall, one could see remarkably bright lights surrounding the city. These were the fires of wagoners who were camping for the night on the edge of town in order to get their goods to the market first thing in the morning.

At sunrise, the market was a bustle of activity. It truly was the heartbeat of Fayetteville.

Even the Town House bell was a city staple. The bell rang numerous times daily, keeping citizens prompt (and in some cases, honest). It played a part in almost every momentous event that happened in the town, such as the welcoming of distinguished guests, calling public gatherings or announcing dramatic news.

Business boomed around the Town House, evident in this 1890–1900 photo. *Courtesy of the North Carolina State Archives.*

Other special bells were the "breakfast" bell at 7:30 a.m., the "dinner" bell at 1:00 p.m., the "sunset" bell at the exact minute of sunset and the "curfew" bell at 9:00 p.m. The curfew was originated as a signal that all slaves must be in their respected quarters. If they were found without a street pass after curfew, they could be put in jail until released by their masters. Children were expected to be indoors before the bell rang.

Local historians wrote about the Town House's many uses. One said:

> *This building over the years meant many things for many people. Underneath its supporting pillars, a shelter for those caught in the winter rain or summer shower; old soldiers tell of their past experience sitting on oak benches which served as a resting place for the weary. But, in order to cherish such remembrances, we must acknowledge the sale of slaves, which did happen here.*

Generally, slaves were only sold to settle estates when a homeowner or landowner passed away with unpaid debts. Truthfully, the number of times a slave was sold at the Town House was few. Rumors and exaggerated stories have unfortunately proliferated over the years.

Mr. Alexander Campbell was born in Fayetteville in 1855 and provided the following narrative shortly before his death:

> *My father was A.M. Campbell and he was City Auctioneer and often sold property at public auction.*
>
> *In 1861 or 1862, my father was in charge of the estate of J.J. Johnson, who was a minor, and my father had charge of some eight or ten slaves belonging to J.J. Johnson. Whenever it was necessary to raise money, my father would sell, under Court order, some property and sometimes a slave.*
>
> *I recall distinctly going one day with Robert Cotton, a slave boy who stayed at my father's house, to the Old Market House where the boy was to be sold at public auction along with several other slaves. The first one sold was a first cousin of Robert and I believe his name was Alec Cotton. This boy was about twenty-one years of age. When he was sold he brought a good price but after the sale the purchaser was told by someone that the boy had a scar on him. The boy showed the purchaser the scar on his knee and the purchaser then refused to make good his bid. We were all mighty glad of it because he was a great musician and a most agreeable boy and a hard worker and we were fond of Alec.*
>
> *The Cotton boy's mother was present when Robert was sold and cried all the time during the sale. The mother prayed soon afterwards that her boy would never do the purchaser any good and we found out soon afterwards that the boy died within two months after the sale. She said afterwards that she was sorry that she made that prayer because the boy might have lived and she could have seen him again.*
>
> *I have seen slaves sold at the Old Market House by other auctioneers. I may say that slaves were never brought to the Old Market House and sold like farm produce or other things. They were sold there only for the purpose of dividing an estate or satisfying a debt. My companionship as a boy with the slaves were some of the most pleasant days of my life and we all seemed to be happy together.*

More often than not, blacks were seen at the market to shop or sell goods with their masters (by whom they were treated quite equally). Some historians even write about slaves eating from the same plate as their masters or playing a banjo and singing for everyone's amusement. While not every citizen was good-hearted in nature, the majority of townsfolk were kind and honest and considered the Town House and marketplace a spot to be enjoyed by everyone, regardless of race.

THE MARQUIS VISITS FAYETTEVILLE

Fayetteville's namesake, French aristocrat and military officer the Marquis de Lafayette, came to America's aid during the Revolutionary War and was an integral part of the Continental army under President George Washington. Many American cities were later named for the marquis; however, the beloved city of Fayetteville was the only one he personally visited.

Lafayette traveled from Raleigh to Fayetteville on March 4, 1825, and he arrived in the city to much pomp and circumstance. The next week, the *Carolina Observer* provided citizens with a vivid account of the marquis' visit. It read:

> *The pride of all hearts and the delight of all eyes, the illustrious American General Lafayette, arrived here on Friday evening last.*
>
> *We cannot pretend to give a regular correct detail of the scenes to which his presence gave rise. The task is far above our ability. Such, however, as is in our power, we must offer our readers:*
>
> *The General entered the town about 5 o'clock...* [and] *proceeded amidst the discharge of artillery, to the Town House, where several hundred persons were assembled, numbers of whom, though the rain continued to descend, as*

The Marquis de Lafayette was the inspiration behind the names of many U.S. cities. Fayetteville, North Carolina, was the only one he personally visited. *Library of Congress Prints & Photographs Division.*

it had done for several days, with little intermission, had patiently awaited the approach of the General, regardless of every consideration of comfort or health. When arrived in front of the Town House, where a spacious stage had been erected for the occasion, the troops formed lines on each side of the street, and the carriages, containing the General and suite, passed between them to the east door of the House, here, alighting from his carriage, with the gentlemen accompanying him, he was met by Judge Toomer, who, in behalf of the Committee and citizens of Fayetteville, welcomed him in the following words, pronounced in the forcible manner for which the Judge is so remarkable.

"General Lafayette—The Congress of the United States, expressing the will of ten millions of people, invited you to our shores, as the Guest of the Nation. Your arrival has hailed as an era in the annals of our country. Wherever you were seen, you were greeted with acclamations. The 15th of August, in each returning year, will be celebrated as a day of jubilee, by the sons of freedom. Already has American genius consecrated your fame. History has recorded the incidents of your eventful life: Oratory has portrayed your character: and Poetry has sung your praise.

The Governor of North Carolina, anticipating the wishes of his constituents, invited you to our state. The invitation was echoed from the mountains to the coast.

My fellow citizens, the inhabitants of Fayetteville, have, also, solicited the honor of a visit. In their behalf, and as their organ, I bid you welcome to our homes. Forty-three years ago, our fathers named this town, to commemorate your achievements, and to express their gratitude. We receive you, with you and exultation, at our family altars, and request your participation in our domestic comforts. We are plain republicans, and cannot greet you with the pomp common on such occasions. Instead of pageantry we offer you cordiality. We have no splendid arches, gilded spires, or gorgeous palaces to present you, but we tender the hospitality of our homes and the grateful homage of devoted hearts."

Judge Toomer went on at length, giving a rousing and extremely welcoming speech to the marquis. Lafayette was warm and receptive, offering the following response to Judge Toomer:

Sir, at every step of my progress through the United States, I am called to enjoy the emotions arising from patriotic feelings and endearing recollections, from the sight of the improvements I witness, and from the affectionate welcomes I have the happiness to receive—those sentiments, Sir, are particularly excited when, upon entering the interesting and prosperous town which has done me the honor to adopt my name, I can at once admire its actual progress and anticipate its future destinies; convinced as I am that the generous and enlightened people of North Carolina will continue all assistance to improve the natural advantages of Fayetteville and make it more and more useful to the State.

Your kind allusions to past times, your flattering commendation of my personal services in our common cause, your remembrance of my peculiar state and connexions [sic], and particularly of my obligations to my gallant Carolinian deliverer, call for my most grateful thanks. The spirit of independence early evinced by the fathers of the young friends, who so kindly accompany me, is highly honorable to that part of the Union. I cordially join in your wishes for the universal emancipation of mankind; and beg you, my dear Sir, and the citizens of Fayetteville, to accept the tribute of my deep and lively gratitude for your so very honorable and gratifying reception.

It was noted that after these two vigorous speeches, the crowd responded with three cheers of huzzah. The Marquis de Lafayette was only in town for about twenty-four hours, half of which was spent under the cover of cloudy skies and rain (as it apparently had been for the past several days).

However, on the morning of the day of his departure, the sun rose in all its brilliant glory, glinting off the waters of the Cape Fear and providing the warmth that only a Carolina sun can offer.

The marquis spent the day visiting with troops that had been with him during the Revolutionary War and later sat down to a formal dinner with 150 guests. In parting, he provided the following toast to the town: "May Fayetteville receive all the encouragements, and obtain all the prosperity, which are anticipated by the fond and grateful wishes of its affectionate and respectful namesake."

During his visit, the marquis stayed at the Hotel Lafayette (also named in his honor). The hotel was completed in 1825, just as the marquis was visiting the town. It was described as a building with "splendid architecture, with quoined [*sic*] corners and heavy square arches." It was a lovely building, nicely furnished (some rooms even had featherbeds), with all the finery of the day.

The Hotel Lafayette remained so popular after that visit that, until 1907, a list of the hotel's guests was printed daily in the *Fayetteville Observer*.

The inscription on this postcard sent in 1910 calls this the "Old Whitefield Residence" and shows the balcony on which General Lafayette spoke while on his American visit. *Courtesy of Larry Tew.*

This modern edition of the Hotel Lafayette was built in 1885 directly next door to the original structure visited by the marquis. *Courtesy of Larry Tew.*

The Good Old Days

The first few decades of the 1800s are often referred to as the "good old days" of Fayetteville, its golden age where people were honest and hardworking. John Oates probably put it best when he said that Fayetteville "merchants were not the progressive men of the 20th century; they were conservative and cautious, and as honest as the day, with their word their bond. They made money slowly, but they lived simply, and gradually accumulated modest fortunes." Fayetteville had become a cultural mecca, with booming business and trade, as well as a lovely place to settle down and raise a family. Its golden age made it unstoppable.

III

THE GREAT FIRE OF 1831

A nd then, it seems, everything was gone.

THE TOWN BURNS

A devastating fire destroyed all of downtown Fayetteville on the afternoon of May 29, 1831. There is a small question of where the fire originated. Some believe the fire began in the kitchen of the house of James Kyle; others believe it was in his smokehouse. In those days, it was not uncommon to have a smokehouse for the curing and storage of meat.

Personal accounts remember the day as being particularly hot and dry, as early summer in North Carolina is wont to be. Newspapers published accounts that "the great heat of the weather was very unfavorable; the sun's rays had heated the roofs of the houses almost to inflammation, and rendered them fit to be ignited by the smallest spark." Not surprisingly, with those conditions, the fire spread quickly. It took a mere six hours and nearly the entirety of downtown was gone—more than six hundred homes and businesses were completely destroyed. Most of the important public buildings were gone, including the Town House, the Cape Fear First Bank, hotels and numerous churches.

One church in particular, the Episcopal Church, housed the town clock in its steeple. It is said that the clock was intent on fulfilling its duty to the very end, as it struck three o'clock as it was burning.

The Great Fire of 1831 started in the Kyle House, seen in this circa 1935 photo. *Library of Congress Prints & Photographs Division.*

Every single home on Maiden Lane and Hay, Anderson, Gillespie, Person, Old, Bow and Green Streets was resolved to blackened brick and ash. Remarkably, no deaths or life-threatening injuries were reported. How the city escaped loss of life in a tragedy of this size is still baffling. Some say the size of the fire and the amount of loss are directly proportional to the Chicago fire of October 1871 when you compare populations.

At the time, there were two news publications in Fayetteville: the *North Carolina Journal* and the *Carolina Observer*. Both were weekly newspapers. Both of their operating buildings were completely destroyed in the fire. Intent on getting the story of the fire published, the two journals merged to print a one-page sheet some two weeks after the fire subdued.

Printed on June 7, 1831, the lengthy account of the fire is accurate, moving and detailed and probably provides the very best description of what happened that fateful day. The story's headline reads, "The editors of the *North Carolina Journal* and *Carolina Observer* unite in giving to their readers the following account of the awful catastrophe of Sunday last. The delay in issuing it has been unavoidable." The story reads:

About 15 minutes after 12 o'clock P.M., on Sunday last, the citizens of Fayetteville were alarmed by the cry of "Fire," and the other signals used on such occasions. The roof of the kitchen belonging to Mr. James Kyle, near his brick building lately erected at the Northwest corner of Market Square, was found to be in blaze, but to so inconsiderable an extent, that it was believe the efforts made to extinguish it would certainly be successful. Deceitful hope! They were all unavailing. In a very few moments the flames extended themselves to the large brick building, and to many small wooden buildings in its vicinity. In a few minutes more the roof of the Town House caught, and that building was soon enveloped in flames. From thence four large torrents of flame were seen pouring in as many directions along the four principal streets of the town with a rapidity and force which defied all stay or resistance.

In a western direction the fire extended itself up Hay Street, and on the right hand a short distance beyond the point of its intersection with Old Street, extending backwards in a northern direction to the very edge of the creek, embracing in its devouring sweep the intermediate buildings on Old Street and Maiden Lane. And on the left as far as Mr. Cannte's wooden building, being the next house below Mr. John McRae's long row of wooden buildings, at the Wagon Yard, extending back southwardly to Franklin Street. Along Green Street the flames progressed northwardly, crossing the creek, and consuming in their transit Mr. Eccle's mill, store and dwelling-house, and the handsome bridge erected a few years since by the town, sweeping before them many valuable buildings, including the Episcopal Church on the right side of the street, until they reached the private residence of James Seawell, Esq., which was saved, by a providential turn of the wind and the active exertions of a very few persons with water and blankets.

On the left hand side of the street they progressed until they were stopped at the house of J.W. Wright, Esq., by blowing it up, and extended back until they reached the house of T.L. Hybart, Esq., which was saved by exertions of great activity and perseverance. Along Person Street they destroyed every building on both sides as far eastwardly as a few doors below Liberty Point, including the store of Mr. Wm. McIntyre, situate

[sic] *on the opposite point formed by the junction of Person Street and Cool Spring Alley, extending back northwardly as far as the edge of the creek, consuming the Presbyterian church, Catholic Chapel, and all the other buildings (with the exception of the dwelling house, mills, and warehouse of Mr. James H. Hooper, all of which were saved with much exertion), including the buildings on both sides of Bow Street.*

Along Gillespie Street, the flames extended as far as the State Bank building, on the right hand side, which being nearly fireproof enabled the citizens to contend successfully with the flames at that point, and to save that building. On the eastern side of the street they destroyed every building to a point opposite the State Bank building, and extending eastwardly so far as to include all but three of the buildings on Dick Street, between Person and Mumford Streets.

It is impossible to form any correct estimate of the entire loss in real estate. There probably is no instance in history of so large a portion of a town being consumed, where it was not the result of voluntary human agency. The fire continued to rage with unabated fury until about six o'clock, when, by the blowing up of houses, and the other means usual on such occasions, it was suddenly deprived of food for its raging appetite.

The public buildings destroyed were, the Town House, the Cape Fear Bank, the Catholic Chapel, the Presbyterian and Episcopal Churches, the [Fayetteville] Academy, the Lafayette and Mansion Hotels. The building in which the United States Bank did business, and the office of the agency of the State Bank, were also destroyed, but as they were merely rented for that purpose, they were not put down as public buildings. The private buildings destroyed, in number about SIX HUNDRED, would require a long catalogue to enumerate particularly.

But besides the buildings, immense quantities of books, valuable papers, money, household furniture, goods, wares, merchandise, and produce, were destroyed. Where the first fire broke out, persons near the scene would remove such things to what were then supposed places of safety, but by the time they would get them fairly deposited they would discover the flames in hot pursuit of them, and would be driven to further efforts for the security of their valuables, until driven from place to place, and completely worn down with their exertions, they would at last be compelled to abandon them to the power of the merciless flames. A very small portion of any of these articles were saved. The amount destroyed it is difficult to estimate. We cannot undertake to offer a correct list of these houses, or even point out the principal sufferers. It would be infinitely more easy to make a catalogue of those of our citizens that have not suffered.

Language is entirely inadequate to the description of the sublime and awful scene of Sunday, or to convey an adequate idea of the appearance of ruin and desolation which our town now presents. If pity was wrung from the iron heart of the stern Marius, a disinterested foreigner, what must be the feelings of every warm hearted citizen of the United States, and especially of our own State, when he shall look upon the melancholy wreck of our late flourishing village?

Continuing on from there, the story finishes by commending those who worked tirelessly and valiantly to extinguish the flames. The newspaper story especially recognized the slaves, commenting on their deserved credit for their conduct: "They all seemed to work with great zeal and intrepidity which manifested a hearty sympathy in the common cause."

In a town of thirty-five hundred residents, a loss of this measure could have been a death sentence. However, as they stand to be today, Fayettevillians are resilient. The townsfolk rallied together to rebuild. Because the fire was so all consuming, this tragedy received national attention.

A local pastor, Henry A. Rowland, wrote letters to the editors of major national papers, as well as letters to be placed in church circulars throughout the country. The following letter was sent to the editor of the *National Gazette*. It was written on the night of the fire. Appropriately so, Rowland's words are raw, emotional and effective:

SIR—FAYETTEVILLE IS NO MORE!—This morning the sun rose upon us in its beauty, and with gladdened hearts we flocked to the churches of our God—now we are in RUINS. But two stores of all that this place contained are standing. The rest are entirely consumed. Nothing but stacks of tottering chimneys remain to tell what we once were.

Except in the outskirts of the town, and in those streets which are a little off from the center of our town, not a dwelling house remains. All the churches, with the exception of the Methodist, which is distant from the center of town, are destroyed. The academy, the two splendid hotels, our printing offices, the two banks, the old state house, every apothecary shop, and some of our mills, are in ashes...

As I wandered through the outskirts of the place to administer relief, so far as possible, to the distressed, my heart sunk within me. The sick were borne out of their houses, and were lying on pallets in the street. Others, faint and exhausted, were reclining on the beds which had been thrown out. Every moment our ears were stunned with the explosion of powder, to demolish the buildings, which might stay the flames. But although many were thus leveled, there was not strength to pull the timers from the reach of the conflagration.

It is impossible to paint the heart rending scenes which every where occurred. Parents were inquiring for their children, and children for their parents, and in every countenance reigned despair.

I have been round the fire in every direction, and the above statements are the result of my own observation. From where I now write I can perceive, for the event of nearly half a mile, the light which flashes up from the smoldering ruins. A very small portion of the property was insured. Most of the people lost their all! Our distress may be partially imagined, but cannot be justly conceived of. Much bodily injury was experienced, but, so far as it is present known, no lives were lost. What results may be ascertained when our friends are collected, it is impossible to say.

Yours with respect,
HENRY A. ROWLAND, Junr.

A similar letter was sent to the editors of the *New-York Journal of Commerce*. Help immediately began to pour into Fayetteville. The outpouring of sympathy from the entire country was overwhelming, even by today's standards. Contributions of all kinds were made to the city. Monetary donations poured in from churches, businesses and individuals from all over the country. Citizens of Boston, New York and Philadelphia contributed more than $10,000 from each city. Even President Andrew Jackson donated $50. When all was said and done, the city had amassed more than $100,000 in monetary donations alone.

A Boston firehouse donated a water-pumping engine. It was considered a prized possession of the Phoenix Fire Company (not chartered until 1834). Named the Yankee, the hand-pumped fire engine was delivered by boat down the Cape Fear River. It arrived in 1832 as rebuilding efforts were in full swing.

After the Great Fire of 1831, Fayetteville was given a hand-pumped fire engine.
This is a photo of the fire brigade around the turn of the twentieth century.
Courtesy of Larry Tew.

Despite this generous gift, it would remain ineffective until the city developed a water system with hydrants capable of supplying hose streams in 1893.

Unfortunately, two more fires occurred in 1845 and 1846, delaying construction projects.

On June 6, 1845, a fire began in a warehouse just north of Hay Street. A number of the buildings destroyed in the Great Fire of 1831 had been rebuilt in brick, but a few (mostly mercantile buildings) were wood. Again, they burned. The fire took fifty-four buildings, about one-third of the still scarred city. Among them was, again, the *Carolina Observer*'s building. Citizens were in an uproar because arson was suspected. A $250 reward was offered for "the person who fired the town."

Barely a year later, on July 22, 1846, a third fire struck the downtown area, destroying roughly thirty stores and a warehouse around the town square. Within a year, nearly all the buildings were rebuilt—this time all in brick.

It seemed Fate had it in her eyes to eradicate Fayetteville, but the city fought back. Fayetteville historian John Oates put it best when he wrote in *The Story of Fayetteville* of the city's resilience:

After the fire, Fayetteville citizens pulled together to rebuild. Most important was the Town House, a town icon. *Library of Congress Prints & Photographs Division.*

However, notwithstanding all her reverses and difficulties innumerable, her people have gone along patiently and persistently doing what they could in a quiet way, always ready and willing to lend a helping hand to others more needy than themselves. We had many energetic men who planned and labored for the good and welfare of the town. Trade poured in, and business flourished; we had many manufactories of various kinds, tanneries, carriage manufactories, shoe factories, cotton factories, four in number in the town, and several in a few miles outside. These gave employment to hundreds of persons. Besides we had mills—flour, grist, and lumber, which kept all busy, and plenty and prosperity reigned. All were happy and comfortable, peaceful and contented.

For many years, the city continued to grow and prosper. The time between the Great Fire and the start of the Civil War is the usual timeline given when referring to the city as antebellum Fayetteville.

IV

ANTEBELLUM FAYETTEVILLE

A fter the rebuilding of its entire downtown, Fayetteville was able to pick up where it left off before the Great Fire. It returned to its distinction as a commercial center, most notably as an early purveyor of cotton and other textiles.

COMMERCE

After the fire, mercantile business began growing again. In 1835, seventy-five of these businesses were listed in Fayetteville tax records, growing to ninety-nine businesses by 1852. These merchants sold any and all kinds of wares, but mostly salt, sugar, molasses, spirits and iron. In 1834, records indicate that 2,284 hogsheads, 3,495 barrels and 373 tierces of merchandise were brought up the Cape Fear River to be sold in stores (along with 349 tons of iron, 1,531 casks of limestone and 80,399 bushels of salt).

Even with all these imports, agriculture was easily the largest industry in town, and it dominated the Cumberland County economy in the 1830s, '40s and '50s. The most prevalent occupations were "planters" and "farmers." While cotton was king, tobacco, grain and cattle played almost as big a role.

Tobacco's role in antebellum industry was at first very large but severely tapered off by the 1840s. For example, by 1792, there were three separate tobacco firms holding warehouses in Fayetteville, in addition to a tobacco

The Town House and the Hotel Lafayette can clearly be seen in this 1890s-era Fayetteville postcard of "Hay Street Looking East." *Courtesy of the North Carolina State Archives.*

factory on the banks of the Cape Fear River. These warehouses had the capability of storing six thousand hogsheads. (In the case of tobacco, a hogshead was a rounded, wooden barrel used to contain tobacco while it was transported or stored. Generally, these containers were approximately fifty gallons in size.)

In 1816, tobacco that was exported from Fayetteville totaled 2,337 hogsheads at a value of more than $400,000. Numbers slowly began to decline while cotton became more and more important. The invention of the cotton gin, and ensuing demand for the product, bolstered Fayetteville's economy. Consequently, cotton was Cumberland County's leading money crop for more than a century, bringing in more than $600,000 a year in 1816.

Unfortunately, as in most farming communities, the economy waxed and waned with the price of cotton. The Panic of 1819 sent the price of cotton from thirty cents a pounds to less than fifteen cents. The price of cotton hit its lowest pre–Civil War point at nine cents a pound after the Panic of 1837. For the next twenty years, prices were in constant flux.

Of the products manufactured in Cumberland County before the war, hats, carriages, saddles and other leather wares, pottery, guns and paper were among the most popular. In fact, the carriage factory belonging to A.A.

McKethan was often described as the largest in the South. It was located in two adjoining brick buildings on the corner of Dick and Person Streets, and in 1856, it employed seventy workers and "shipped 20 custom-made buggies to southern states in the last twelve months."

Fayetteville historian Quincy Scarborough printed somewhat of a roster of antebellum "artists and artisans" in Cumberland County, and it gives a good representation of the businesses established in Fayetteville. He lists eight artists; five gunsmiths; four potters; twenty-seven cabinetmakers, joiners and chair makers; four house and ornamental painters; seven metalworkers; three tinsmiths; twenty-five silversmiths and watchmakers; three upholsterers; and two stonecutters, among others. Antebellum business in Fayetteville was certainly booming.

FARMING

One of Cumberland County's most prominent farmers, James Evans, lived and worked the fields of Fayetteville before the war. He and his wife, Martha, had eleven children, and Evans occasionally wrote essays for the *Fayetteville News*. His diaries belong to the Southern Historical Collection at the University of North Carolina at Chapel Hill. His writings provide a good representation of what life was like on the antebellum farm. A few excerpts read:

> *1851: We had a hard frost on Friday March 21/51 ice a plenty, in fact the Sump* [a hole built to collect water] *was froze hard we had to pour hot water in it to thaw it. Peach trees in full bloom. Friday night quite cloudy—rained on Saturday & turned quite warm…on 15 we had considerable frost on the 22nd we had some frost, & on the 23rd we had a hoary frost, weather quite dry, consequently no serious injury—Aug 15 peaches & apples very plenty.*

> *1853: We had a real snow storm on the 5 March 1853…We planted Irish Potatoes on Good Friday the 25 of March/53—June 15 complete failure, drought. We bedded slips on the 30 of March, sprouted very well. No rain in May till 24 June. Commenced planting corn Apr. 1 & finished on the 30 Apr. Corn up awful bad, it being decidedly the drought & the coldest spring I ever saw. Planted peas June 15. Sept 20 quite considerable.*

1854: We planted oats on the 13, 14, & 15 March. It being too wet to plant them sooner. We planted some 31 March. Corn cut July 4. We planted Irish Potatoes on the 14 Mar. June 20 very good! Dug them all by July 27, Very good. We bedded slips on the 31 May. Aug 1 They look very well Sept 1—proved good!

Winter/spring 1857: Ellick died on the 8 of Dec/56—3 o'clock A.M.

Summer 1857: It is the general belief that this had been by far the coldest, most disagreeable & backward spring we ever had. Mulberries are very Scarce, & have just commenced ripening—my best corn is about 8 inches high—generally about 4. I am not done seeding corn—The weather is very dry & the corn is missing badly—No potatoes set out, though the sprouts look well—I have no oats—but other peoples are about a foot high—The prospect generally, is decidedly bad. But oh! The flower Garden is filled with the choicest roses, & all nature is perfumed with thin fragrance…

1859: We commenced hauling manure of the 18 Apr 1859 & Finished on the 28—We planted the Flat swamp piece on the 16 Apr & the New ground about it, on the 30…May 5 planted 2 low land & would have finished planting corn on the 7 but the ground was so dry & hard we had to stop—we picked a qt of ripe huckleberries on the 5—We had a little Shower on the Evening of the 10 & I planted sugar corn, pop corn & water melon seed in the orchard on the 11.

BANKING

Between 1804 and 1933, Fayetteville operated twenty-five banks (twenty state and five national); however, the antebellum era of banking was certainly one of the most profitable and economically stimulating.

In 1849, the Bank of Fayetteville was chartered, and the General Assembly of North Carolina incorporated it in the same year. Numerous banks operated in Fayetteville at the time, but few saw such a high capital (the Bank of Fayetteville's capital stock was $800,000). Fayetteville began influencing the state's economic life as offshoot branches were opened in Wadesboro, Greensboro, Salisbury and Washington, North Carolina.

This early twentieth-century view of the National Bank of Fayetteville shows its location on the corner of Hay and Green Streets. *Courtesy of Larry Tew.*

Chester S. Davis wrote *The Story of Carolina Banking,* describing North Carolina bankers:

> *The story of banking in North Carolina is the story of hard working men, who make their living by carrying the public's money down the trail. When financial skies are sunny the banker has been pictured as a stout and solid fellow, a pillar in the community. But when the skies are leaden, the banker has not been so popular. As he stumbled along the uncertain trail he has been lampooned as a greedy, stingy man who oozed gold and greenbacks from less fortunate comrades. But regardless of fickle public favor, the banker has plowed along, doing what he could to better his community.*

And that is exactly the nature of bankers in Fayetteville. Bank heads were generally well-known members of the community whose family names leave legacies.

The Cumberland National Bank replaced the National Bank of Fayetteville on the corner of Hay and Green Streets. *Courtesy of Larry Tew.*

When the Bank of Fayetteville opened, the *Fayetteville Observer* printed an advertisement listing all the names of bank heads. It read:

The Bank of Fayetteville has for its President, John D. Williams, Sr., a gentleman whose name in the commercial world insures the confidence of a watchful and cautious people, with John C. Haigh, Jr., the embodiment of honor as cashier, and W.G. Broadfoot, cashier, J.H. Marsh, teller, Ed. Lilley, bookkeeper, G.G. Myrover, clerk, in all of whom the people will have the utmost confidence. The Directors are James Kyle, John D. Starr, Henry Lilly, James Martine, and John T. Gilmore.

Of course, a business like banking can hardly be expected to maintain a spotless image. A bank robbery in Fayetteville marred the squeaky-clean image of the day's banks (but certainly did provide plenty for the gossips of yore to talk about).

Fayetteville's very first bank, a branch of the Cape Fear Bank, opened in 1807 with John Hogg as president and John Winslow and John Wright as cashiers. About the same time, a man by the name of Alexander Gray moved to town, seemingly out of the blue. An 1893 account titled *Traditions of Cross Creek and Reminiscences of Fayetteville*, written by Robert Cochran Belden and published by the *Fayetteville Observer*, reads:

> *He was a man of polished manners and pleasing address, but there was an air of mystery about him that caused suspicion, and people could not understand why, without family and nothing apparently to do, he should lead so secluded a life.*

One day soon thereafter, Mr. Wright approached the bank's vault, either to make a deposit or simply as part of his rounds. He noticed something strange: there were small bits of wax around the vault's keyhole. Through some roundabout logic, it was determined that Alexander Gray had, late one night, entered the bank through the cellar door, gained access to the vault room and, with wax, taken an impression of the keyhole. A sting operation was set up in an effort to catch Mr. Gray red-handed.

There was a warehouse to the rear of the bank, directly facing the cellar doors. It was decided that Mr. Wright and a few others would spend a few nights camped out in the warehouse, each taking turns watching for Mr. Gray to come back. The same old account said that "the plan agreed upon was to let Gray open and enter the cellar, give him some time, then rushing out secure the burglar."

The first few nights were unsuccessful, but on the last planned night of the sting, Wright and his comrades saw a figure in the dark. They watched as the figure approached the cellar door, raised his lantern to check for onlookers, opened the door and snuck in. The plan was to wait a few minutes, but the wait was not needed. For some unknown reason, Gray climbed out of the cellar almost as soon as he had entered it and fled the scene.

As the story goes, "On the same night the store of John Mullins was entered, some money and a few articles of small value were taken. Mullins, suspecting Gray, swore out a search warrant. His house was examined and the missing property was found."

Alexander Gray was arrested, tried at the next superior court and convicted of the crimes. Later that week, Gray and one other criminal were hanged in the gallows on the grounds of the U.S. Arsenal.

POLITICS

In addition to industry and banking, Fayetteville was a hotbed of political activity in the years before the Civil War.

Cumberland County voters had always been very active, flooding the polls on election days and generally being highly participatory in campaigns. The 1820s saw the advent of the "Second American Party System," and Fayetteville voters found themselves avidly supporting Andrew Jackson. From then on, it seemed that citizens were sharply divided between the Democratic and Whig Parties. Every election between 1834 and 1860 saw active participation and spirited campaigning in town.

At that time, campaigning entailed many things. Anything from rallies and parades to newspaper advertisements and dizzyingly long diatribes could be expected during campaign season. The Town House was often the site of hours-long debates between candidates.

The election of 1834 was especially spirited and is recounted in John Oates's book *The Story of Fayetteville and the Upper Cape Fear*. Thomas L. Hybart (Democrat) and James Seawell (Whig) were the candidates, and the two held meetings almost nightly. For "weeks before the election, balls were given by the Whigs in [an] old tobacco warehouse...There Saxons and dusky maids danced to the music of the banjo." Apparently, the main goal of the dances was to gain the vote of free blacks, of which Fayetteville had a large population, as they were the main attendants of the dances.

The story of the election goes on to say that "never had the old borough witnessed such excitement as on the day of election." Those eligible to vote were legal residents who had lived in Fayetteville for more than twelve months; however, people with shorter terms and those with freeholds were also voting. The problems this caused is the real reason the election of 1834 is so memorable.

Supposedly, the Whig Party tried to stack its votes by extorting freeholds. At the time, any landowner could vote. A freehold was a partial division of a lot of land, regardless of size, that could be purchased in order to vote. The patch of land could honestly only be large enough for a man to stand in but could still be considered his private property, making him eligible to vote. Fictitious titles were made by the subdivision of lots into freeholds, resulting in a Democratic win. This gave rise to a heated debate that,

> *except for a conciliatory speech made by Edward Winslow, would have brought on bloodshed. An inflammatory speech by Louis Henry and a retort by Edward Hale led to a difficulty between those gentlemen, which, though composed by friends, were indicative of the unhappy effect of this election upon the social life of Fayetteville.*

Regardless of citizens' approval of those in office, the town government provided a sense of order in Fayetteville. While political activity was great and citizens may have debated issues concerning the United States as a whole, the people of Fayetteville generally agreed on what could be called "internal improvements"—essentially anything to do with boosting the city's economy. The town's elected officials consisted of seven commissioners selected from determined wards, as well as a "magistrate of police" (later given the title of mayor in 1857). All of these positions were elected on an annual basis and served to regulate the town as best as they could.

The most notable politicians to come out of antebellum Fayetteville were William Barry Grove (five-time Federalist congressman), Louis D. Henry (the 1842 Democratic candidate for governor) and other young leaders such as James Dobbin, Warren Winslow and Jesse Shepherd.

THE END OF AN ERA

As they say, all good things must come to an end. Whispers of war were perhaps the only things that shook Fayetteville to its core. Never one to sit back and rest on its laurels, Fayetteville was on the front lines, armed and ready, when the War Between the States erupted.

V
THE CIVIL WAR

With war in the wind, Fayetteville tried earnestly to maintain some semblance of normalcy. Little did residents know that their idea of normal was going to be drastically different for the next five years than any season they had yet experienced.

WARTIME

Fayetteville has had a hand in almost every major conflict of the modern world, and the Civil War was no exception. The location of the Fayetteville Arsenal made the city pivotal to the Confederacy, as it was the center of the manufacture of arms for the government. The arsenal was overtaken by the Confederacy in 1861.

Originally, Fayetteville (and most of North Carolina) had no interest in secession. As a slave state, one-third of North Carolina's population in 1860 was slave. Abraham Lincoln was elected president in 1860 under the platform of opposing the expansion of slavery into territories owned by the United States. He received no votes from North Carolina. After his election, Southern slaveholding states seceded from the Union, thus creating the Confederate States of America in opposition to the Republicans' position against the expansion of slavery.

In February 1861, a statewide referendum issued a call for a convention to consider secession. North Carolina voters were split almost evenly, with the Cumberland County votes reflecting almost the same statistics. The state saw 46,672 in favor of the convention and 47,333 against it. Cumberland County voted 1,038 for and 959 against—extremely slim margins by anyone's standard. With the state refusing secession, North Carolina then sent representatives to Washington, D.C., in an attempt to draw up peaceful negotiations between Northern and Southern leaders. It was unsuccessful, and North Carolina did not secede until President Lincoln requested 75,000 troops to fight against rebelling Southern states. On May 20, 1861, North Carolina was one of the last of the Confederate states to withdraw from the Union.

Just after Lincoln's call for arms, a militia company commanded by Colonel John H. Cook marched to the arsenal under instruction by North Carolina's governor, John Ellis. Colonel Cook called on Captain James Bradford to surrender the arsenal to the state, and he did so. A North Carolina flag was raised over the arsenal, and Bradford joined the Southern army as an artilleryman.

It took just a few short weeks for several hundred young men to join military companies. The steamboat *A.P. Hurt* busily ferried soldiers up and down the Cape Fear River from Fayetteville to Wilmington. From Wilmington, the recruits took railroad cars to regimental gathering places like Raleigh, and by the fall, they were fighting.

During all this time, the whole of Fayetteville (and especially the arsenal) was preparing itself for action.

On February 23, 1862, Fayetteville citizen Robert Fuller was chosen to go to Richmond to meet with the Confederate government about plans for the defense of the city of Fayetteville. Fuller was also responsible for acquiring small arms and ammunition to defend the stretch of the Cape Fear River that ran through town. He was awarded $100 to use toward these expenses.

The following day, with the capture of the Cape Fear becoming more and more imminent, city commissioners formed a committee of safety. Notable members of the committee were H. Myrover, E. Hale, Dr. Ben Robinson, Charles Haigh, E.J. Lilly, W. Broadfoot and James Kyle. As it turns out, the committee of safety never saw an official battle, though it did impose lofty regulations on townsfolk. For example, on March 17, 1862, the committee ordered that no cotton, turpentine, spirituous liquors or rosin were to be stored within town limits (unless citizens had express permission from the authorities). This was done with the thought that armies would stay away from Fayetteville because there was nothing of value to be taken within its limits. Turpentine or no turpentine, the war continued.

Days of fighting turned into weeks, then into months and then into years—five Aprils paid in blood and futures. Fayetteville resident Melinda Ray was a teenager during the war and kept quite a detailed diary filled mostly with sad details of death. One entry reads, "James Huske was killed near Petersburg Oct. 27th. He has been in the war since the commencement of it. His mother, a widow, is left desolate. She had two sons three years ago, and now they are both gone."

Fayetteville citizen William Graham wrote the following letter to his girlfriend, Winnie Blount, who was waiting back home. Graham wrote the letter from Egypt Hospital after suffering an injury:

My Dearest Winnie,
I am in great trouble about one of my friends who was killed in Bentonsville last week, Mr. McNeill. I know you have heard me speak of him frequently. He was one of the best young men I ever met with…Poor fellow the last time I saw him was below Wilmington. When I got hurt, he took all of my things and brought me almost to Wilmington or till he got a wagon to take me. Oh it makes tears come to my eyes to think of it. He was such a noble young man. He has done more for me than any man in my Co. He fell just at the moment the Yankee beast, they had taken one and he was in advance of the rest of the regiment some 20 or 30 yards and just before he fell he looked back and said, "Come on boys we will soon make them skeedaddle" just then the fatal Ball struck him down falling on his face and never moving. Poor fellow I hope he is at rest and out of this world of war and bloodshed…
Will rest for a while—William Graham, April 13, 1863

Not only were Fayetteville's citizens suffering heartache, but also the city itself suffered as the market fell apart and prices were severely inflated, due in part to poor monetary policies by the Confederacy, as well as things like the Tariff of Abominations. The main goal of the tariff was to protect Northern industry, which was being put out of business by the low prices of imported goods. The Union began taxing imported goods. This harmed the South especially because it had to pay higher prices for things it simply couldn't produce itself.

Additionally, the exportation of goods to Britain was cut, thus affecting North Carolina's biggest export: cotton. While little money was flowing into the city, prices were also rising, causing some of the greatest economic hardships townspeople had ever seen. Some reports state that things like bacon, which had sold for ten cents a pound before the war, cost six dollars a pound in 1865. Banks were closing in almost domino effect, businesses were failing and, to boot, soldiers were ransacking homes.

A Fayetteville farmer wrote the following vivid account:

Soldiers searched my house from garret to cellar, and plundered it of everything potable; took all my provisions, emptied the pantries of all stores, and did not leave me a mouthful of any kind of supplies for one meal's victuals. They took all my clothing, even the hat off my head, and the shoes and pants from my person. They destroyed my furniture and robbed all my negroes.

And for what? Control, it seemed. From the day Captain Bradford removed the United States flag from the arsenal, it became a beacon for the Confederate army—and a must-have for Union troops. Throughout the war, the arsenal manufactured and stored weapons and ammunition. All of this work was overseen by William Bell, and he was able to send a steady supply of rifles, pistols, ammunition and artillery to the battlefronts. At the beginning of the war, Bell directed eighty or ninety workers. That number bloomed to over two hundred by the end of the war. Some paid workers, but most volunteers, they worked the arsenal's sheds, shops, engine houses and forges.

The arsenal was captured and torched during Sherman's occupation of the South in 1865. William Bell was seventy-two years old and proclaimed that, as he watched his life's work go up in flames, he would never recover. He died not six months later. During Reconstruction, some stones from the ruins were used in rebuilding homes. To this day, some of the original foundation is still in place.

FAYETTEVILLE'S WAR EFFORT

Cornelia Phillips Spencer was a North Carolina historian, poet and journalist. In 1866, she wrote *The Last Ninety Days of the War in North Carolina*, providing stirring accounts and revealing interviews of Sherman's March. She wrote of Fayetteville's contribution to the war effort:

As to Fayetteville, and her lot in these later days, no such slight sketch as this will suffice for her story. Perhaps no town in the South had surpassed her in the ardor and liberality with which (after succession had become the law of the State) she supported the war. She gave her bravest sons; her best blood was poured out like water in the cause of the South, and then she gave of her substance.

Spencer wrote of the citizens' (and especially the women's) devotion to city, state and the Confederacy:

The ladies, as usual, were especially active and indefatigable. Where, indeed, in all the sunny South were they not? And why should they not have been? They were working for their fathers, husbands, sons, brothers, and lovers, and for principles which these loved ones had instructed them to cherish.

Fayetteville supported the Confederate government "warmly to the last gasp, upon the principle that *united,* the South might stand—*divided,* she certainly would fall," Spencer wrote.

The compliments she paid to Fayetteville and its citizens, despite the serious subject matter in which they were administered, should truly be cherished.

SHERMAN

No matter the kindhearted acts of the citizens of Fayetteville, it was still ransacked and burned. Throughout several months, General William T. Sherman's army of sixty thousand marched across the Southern countryside. They stopped in Fayetteville for only a weekend, but that weekend was riddled with destruction never before seen.

General Sherman completed his infamous March to the Sea in December 1864 after his capture of Savannah, Georgia. He set his sights next on Richmond, Virginia, so that he could combine forces with Union general in chief Ulysses S. Grant. Sherman had to get there first. On February 1, Sherman had his sights set on the Carolinas, specifically Fayetteville. He intended to destroy the arsenal, which was essentially the only remaining source of arms for the Confederates. He burned everything in his path. It is said that smoke from Sherman's March slowly rolled up the sky. For

General William T. Sherman terrorized the South, Fayetteville included, during his infamous march. *Library of Congress Prints & Photographs Division.*

hundreds of miles, nearly every home and fencepost was left ablaze. Nearly every citizen in his path was left panic-stricken.

Attempts had been made by numerous Confederate armies to thwart Sherman's march. No one was successful in stopping his advancing armies (or even Sherman's cohort, the Union cavalry commanded by General Judson Kilpatrick, deemed Sherman's "left wing"), but they were successful in temporarily delaying them.

The cavalry under General Kilpatrick was camping a few miles outside Fayetteville, hoping to intercept and overtake any Confederate armies trying to derail Sherman. The plan was to thwart armies passing through on the morning of March 10; however, Confederate armies arrived earlier than expected.

On the evening of March 9, the Confederate cavalry commanded by General Wade Hampton attacked the camp and was successful in running out the Union armies. One horseman rode right up to the house where

General Judson Kilpatrick sometime during the Civil War. *Library of Congress Prints & Photographs Division.*

General Kilpatrick was staying (entertaining a "lady friend," legend has it) just as the general was coming out to flee. He mounted a horse and rode off in the other direction wearing only his underclothes. This incident would later be referred to as "Kilpatrick's Shirttail Skedaddle," though General Kilpatrick was so embarrassed he denied that the event occurred at all.

Union armies were able to retake their camp, but they were not able to slow Confederate forces from reaching Fayetteville before Sherman. General Hardee and his corps reached the town mere hours before Union troops. Attempts to slow or stop Sherman's armies were made by crossing the Cape Fear River and then burning the Clarendon Bridge (a critical thoroughfare to Raleigh in the North).

In a March 7 order issued by Sherman, with his sights set on Fayetteville, he requested that Fayetteville citizens meet his armies with no resistance and, most importantly, that the Clarendon Bridge be left alone. As Sherman said, "If the people will spare the bridge, I want all to be easy on the citizens, but if they burn bridges or bother us we must go the whole figure…Deal as moderately and fairly by the North Carolinians as possible, and fan the flame of discord already subsisting between them and their proud cousins of South Carolina." Sherman did not meet the actions of Hardee's men lightly. In some respects, it made Fayetteville fare much, much worse.

The night before Sherman arrived in Fayetteville, he and his troops camped in the town of Raeford (just four miles southwest of town). He stayed at Bethel Presbyterian Church. After he left, the church's pastor, a Mr. McNeill, found an inscription in the church Bible written by Sherman. It read:

> *Mr. McNeill will please preach a sermon on the illusions of pleasure & hope*
> *Mr. McNeill will please prove the absurdity of the Universalist doctrine*
> *Mr. McNeill will please preach a sermon from the First Epistle of John 4ᵗʰ Chapter*
> *Mr. McNeill will please pray for Old Abe*
> *By Order of*
> *W.T. Sherman*
> *Maj. Genl. Cmd.*
> *U.S. Forces*

After leaving this somewhat sarcastic inscription, the general left Raeford.

Sherman descended on Fayetteville the morning of March 11 with relatively little resistance, except for a few rounds fired off by sharpshooters. His entire divisions of the Fourteenth and Seventeenth Corps entered the city, each one in turn receiving a surrender of Fayetteville from Mayor Archibald McLean.

Once Sherman had possession of the city, he immediately set out to rebuild bridges across the Cape Fear River so that his armies could continue marching toward Goldsboro. He also had Kilpatrick's men destroy specific facilities such as "railroad trestles, depots, mills, and factories." He ordered other high-ranking officials to demolish other important structures. For example, chief ordnance officer T.G. Baylor was responsible for destroying "all power and ordnance stores, including guns and small arms" armories.

Sherman's forces overtook the arsenal and set up camp there. In a letter probably written from the arsenal grounds, General Sherman wrote to General

This pen-and-ink sketch depicts the military corps entering Fayetteville during the Civil War. *Courtesy of the North Carolina State Archives.*

Grant about his actions: "Since I cannot leave a guard to hold it, I therefore shall burn it, blow it up with gunpowder, and then with rams knock down its walls." And that he did. Obliging Colonel O.M. Poe with the responsibility, Sherman charged him with the "utter demolition of the arsenal building and everything pertaining to it." Fayetteville, so used to fire, burned again.

Eyewitnesses wrote accounts of the burning. Fayetteville native Alice Campbell wrote:

> *The nights were made hideous with smoke. The crowning point to this nightmare of destruction was the burning and battering down of our beautiful and grandly magnificent Arsenal, which was our pride, and the showplace of our town.*

As Cornelia Spencer recalled:

> *So adroitly had every house in the town and its suburbs been ransacked and plundered, that it may be doubted if all Fayetteville, the next day, could have contributed two whole shirts or a bushel of meal to the relief of the Confederate army.*

One particular incident about which she wrote was the accosting of William Hooper. Spencer wrote of "Soldiers in Blue" entering the town and accosting citizens. One in particular was clergyman Reverend William Hooper, who was more than seventy years old. The grandson of one of the signers of the Declaration of Independence, Hooper had a pistol put to his head while Union troops demanded and carried off his watch and purse.

This incident infuriated Spencer. In her words:

> *Southerners can not write calmly of such scenes yet. Their houses were turned into seraglios, every portable article of value, plate, china and glass-ware, provisions and books were carried off, and the remainder destroyed; hundreds of carriages and vehicles of all kinds were burned in piles; where houses were isolated they were burned; women were grossly insulted, and robbed of clothing and jewelry; nor were darker and nameless tragedies wanting in lonely situations.*

And so, for nearly two days, the streets of Fayetteville were pillaged.

As quickly as he had come, Sherman was gone, leaving a path of destruction and desolation. Also during that time (the month of March), straggling Confederate soldiers were coming from all parts of the state to converge under General Johnson in Raleigh and Colonel Alfred Rhett just to the south. Some passed through Fayetteville, and despite the fact that it had been so totally accosted, its citizens were as welcoming as they could be.

"The whole population of our town poured out to see these war-torn men; to cheer them; to feed and shelter them," Spencer remembered.

> *The little children gathered handfuls of the early daffodils "that take the winds of March with beauty," and flung to them. What we had to eat we gave them, day after day. Repeatedly the whole of a family dinner was taken from the table and carried out to the street, the children joyfully assisting. They were our soldiers—our own brave boys. The cause was desperate, we knew—the war was nearly over—our delusions were at and end; but while we had it, our last loaf to our soldiers—a cheer, and a blessing, with dim eyes, as they rode away.*

What Sherman didn't know, however, was that upon leaving Fayetteville, his reign was about to be cut short. After a day's march from Fayetteville, Sherman found himself in Averasboro, North Carolina. The retreating Southern soldiers had been camping there and brought a sudden, calculated attack on Sherman and his troops.

Soldiers under the command of Colonel Rhett formed three defensive lines with the intention of cutting off advancing Union cavalry at the head. At this point in the war, the Union cavalry commanded by General Kilpatrick contained thirty thousand soldiers and was considered to be Sherman's left wing (if not also his left hand). When Kilpatrick and his men came upon the Confederate forces, they fought them back to their original defensive line. Confederate reinforcements halted Kilpatrick's advancements, and the skirmish was quiet by nightfall.

The next morning, heavy fighting occurred between the Confederate and Union troops. This fighting resulted in the loss of over 220 Confederate soldiers (either killed, wounded or captured), causing the withdrawal of the Confederate's first and second defensive lines. As the Confederates withdrew pressure, General Sherman pressed on, preparing to attack the third defensive line. They were decisively stopped—and with significant casualties at that—by Confederate general Joe Wheeler's dismounted cavalry. The Union army attempted several attacks throughout the night but found no success.

On the morning of March 17, General Sherman fully anticipated a major assault. However, defending Confederate general William Hardee realized his success in delaying the advance of Sherman's left wing and swiftly withdrew his troops under the cover of darkness. They marched to Bentonville to join General Johnson and his army, with the intention of surprising Sherman again, thus beginning the Battle of Bentonville on March 19, 1865. The war was in its last hours.

General Sherman's actions were not soon forgotten. On March 11, 1920, the *Fayetteville Observer* published a fifty-fifth-anniversary story recapping Sherman's visit to Fayetteville, offering more information than some history books. It read:

On March 11, 1865—55 years ago today—General Sherman and his army, on their celebrated "march to the sea," entered Fayetteville. Rapidly retreating before them, General Hardee's Confederate army occupied part of two days in passing through the town. Hardee burned the Clarendon Bridge across Cape Fear river when all of his army, except a small detachment of Hampton's cavalry, had crossed to the east side.

The entry into and passage through the town of the two armies was widely different. Hardee's came as a friend, though a fleeing one. His soldiers were ragged, worn down and hungry, but they retained much of the fire and spirit for which the southern soldiers were noted. They were received with open arms by the citizens of Fayetteville, and the good women, though the larders of most of them were far from well supplied, handed to the soldiers as they marched by, bread and whatever else in the way of eatables they could scrape together.

Sherman came as a conquering enemy. His soldiers were flushed with victory. They were hearty and strong, having lived off the fat of the land during their march. Hardee's men, as a rule, respected the rights of the people through whose country they passed, leaving untouched provisions and valuables which were later seized by Sherman's "bummers."

...Sherman destroyed the arsenal on Haymount, and those living in that neighborhood will never forget the scenes of that trying day. The engineer corps razed the large and handsome government buildings, using railroad rails as battering rams with which to demolish the walls. When the ruin was complete the debris was set afire and the heat, flames, smoke and general confusion was terrifying to the women and children.

In 1865, Fayetteville was left with a choice: it could bend and break to the dire circumstances that befell it, having been beaten and burned time and time again, or it could rise from the ashes as it had done so many times before. Ever resilient and steadfast, reconstruction efforts began in Fayetteville without a backwards glance.

VI

RECONSTRUCTION

North Carolina was readmitted to the Union on July 4, 1868, after adopting a new constitution giving blacks the right to vote. From there, the months and years after the Civil War were dedicated to rebuilding and bettering Fayetteville for future generations. After more fires and destruction than citizens cared to remember, the city of Fayetteville had grown accustomed to rebuilding. It was something that was in their blood, something they did with pride.

FAYETTEVILLE REMEMBERS

While their main focus was moving on, Fayetteville residents still wanted to make sure that their long journey was not forgotten. None took on this task more than Mrs. Anna K. Kyle (no doubt a relation of the infamous Kyle family in whose house started the fire of 1831). Mrs. Kyle served as a nurse during the war, and soon after General Sherman left Fayetteville, she established the Confederate Burial Ground. Located adjunct to Cross Creek Cemetery (founded in 1785), this selected spot can be found at the back of the cemetery, looking out over Cross Creek.

When the war ended, Mrs. Kyle and a group of Fayetteville women took it upon themselves to erect a monument to honor the Confederate dead. The women needed funding, so they decided to raffle off a homemade silk quilt. Tickets for the raffle were $1 each. The raffle raised $300, and the quilt was eventually given to former Confederate president Jefferson Davis. When Davis died, his wife donated the quilt to the Confederate Museum in Richmond, Virginia, where it still rests in the North Carolina Room.

The monument was to be made of marble from the marble yard of George Lauder, the most productive stonecutter in North Carolina in the 1880s. Lauder is also buried in Cross Creek Cemetery.

Finally erected in 1868, the Confederate monument is the oldest of its kind in the South. It bears the inscription:

> *On Fame's eternal camping ground,*
> *There silent tents are spread.*
> *Rest on embalmed and sainted dead,*
> *Dear as the blood you gave.*

The following poem was written by a Fayetteville citizen just after the end of the Civil War. It is often mentioned in conjunction with the building and dedication of the Confederate monument. The author is unknown.

"War Days in Fayetteville"

> *'Tis a witness how secession*
> *Threw the glove down to oppression*
> *Scorning at the last, concession,*
> *Giving life blood for the right.*
> *Oh, we cannot, cannot lose it,*
> *(Oh how could the world refuse it?)*
> *Can we let the foe abuse it*
> *Or its history bright?*
> *No, in our hearts deep, deep recesses*
> *Its memory lingers yet, and blesses*
> *Those who for it fought and died.*
> *And we pray the God of Heaven*
> *Who our darling idol's given*
> *And who to us this hope has given*
> *That this prayer be not denied*
> *In future years some hand may take it*

From its resting place and shake it
O'er the young and brave,
And the old spirit still undaunted.
In their young hearts by God implanted
Will triumph o'er foes who vaunted
And freedom to the South be granted,
Though now there's none to save.
Though folded now away so sadly
In future years we'll wave it gladly,
In prosperous path we'll tread.
And thousands yet un-born shall hail it,
Tens of thousands never fail it,
For-gotten be the men who wail it—
Hated those that now can trail it—
Oh, can our hopes be dead?

Twenty-five years passed before the thought of erecting another monument was raised. As is written in Oates's book, "Another band of patriotic women were inspired to build a more pretentious monument to the Confederate soldier." The monument was placed at the intersection of four major thoroughfares in town—Ramsey, Green, Grove and Rowan Streets—and bore the inscription, "They died in defense of Right, For them all fall the tears of a Nation's Grief." After just a few short years, the monument had to be moved due to traffic. The new location included an encompassing fence and sidewalks. The following ode was written for the occasion:

"Carolina's Dead"
By Miss Sarah Ann Tillinghast, written for the unveiling of the Cumberland
County Confederate Monument, May 10, 1902

Uncoffined on the battle-field,
Those dreamless ones are sleeping,
Unconscious of the memories
Left in hearts that still are weeping—
Weeping for those that never came—
Brother, and friends, and lovers,
Those gallant ones whose precious forms

Virginia's soil now covers.
Their memory to us is dear;
Virginia too should love them,
For with their blood her fields are soaked,
Tho' now so green above them.
Where they were needed, there they came,
Lee "could not do without them"
And never on a fair fought field
Could foreign valor rout them.
Oh Tennessean hillsides fair,
Alas, how thick they're lying!
And Pennsylvania's rocky heights
Witnessed their faith undying—

This Confederate monument, the second of its kind in Fayetteville, was erected in 1894 at the intersection of Ramsey, Green, Grove and Rowan Streets. *Courtesy of Larry Tew.*

Faith in their cause, which made their wills
So strong they ne'er did falter
In giving life—'twas all they had—
To lay on freedom's altar.

RECESSION

During the Civil War, the economy surged and grew quickly, both from wartime spending and from industrial growth spurred on by the war. Cities all over the country were booming, but when the war ended (consequently ending the need to spend money on it), economies crashed. These recessions were often called panics because they began when people literally panicked at the state of affairs. Fayetteville was not immune to these panics in any way.

As soldiers returned home, they found overgrown farmlands, little trade, no money and no slave labor. Unaccustomed to these changes, Fayetteville's financial situation continued to plummet. At Fayetteville's lowest in August 1865, the city decided to issue paper money, called scrip pay, to its citizens, receivable for taxes and other dues to the town. The paper bills were issued in five-, ten- and twenty-five-cent values. Very little is known about the extent to which (if at all) the money was circulated.

Several more measures were taken in an effort to bolster the town's economic status. For example, part of the town's reconstruction effort was put toward beautifying the town square. Of course, townsfolk were taxed for this purpose. Brick and stone road pavements and curbs were ordered constructed on all the streets leading from the Town House; the curbs were to begin twelve feet from the walls of the buildings. Starting on Person Street, property owners were forced to pay for these improvements.

The city contracted Lauda and Stratton to put down the curb and lay the bricks. The fee was fifty cents per lineal yard for the curbstone and twenty-five cents per square yard for pavements, all to be paid by those who owned the property on which this was happening. As can be imagined, this was not received totally graciously by townsfolk, who did not want to be forcibly taxed out of money they really did not have in the first place.

Taxes on vehicles and loads were also levied. In February 1866, the charge for a vehicle carrying passengers was fifty cents to cross the river and then come back again. The charge for a passenger and his trunk to go to and from the railroad to any part of town (except across the river) was twenty-five cents.

The following year, a schedule of drayage charges was drawn up. From the river, a bale of cotton cost twenty cents, a keg of nails cost ten cents and hides cost five cents each. To the river, a barrel of rosin was twelve and a half cents, a barrel of flour was ten and a half cents and one thousand bricks cost two dollars. It also seems that the rates uphill from the river cost more than the rates downhill.

Despite the fact that the charges were largely unpopular and confusing, they continued to be levied in an attempt to pull Fayetteville out of the economic slump in which it found itself.

FAYETTEVILLE LOSES ITS CHARTER

Eventually, the town's debt grew so large that the General Assembly of North Carolina met to discuss its options. In 1881, Chapter 58 of the Private Laws of 1881 was passed, providing for a compromise of the indebtedness of the City of Fayetteville, conditionally surrendering its charter. It read:

> *An Act to Authorize and Empower the Town of Fayetteville to Compromise its Indebtedness.*
>
> *Whereas, The debt of the town of Fayetteville is so great that it cannot be paid in full; And Whereas, To enforce collection of the same would be very burdensome and cause great distress among the citizens of said town: And Whereas, in all proper cases it is the duty of the sovereign to afford all proper constitutional relief. The General Assembly of North Carolina do Enact: Section 1. That the committee of finance for Fayetteville are authorized and empowered to compromise and settle the bonded indebtedness and interest thereon of said town, by issuing new bonds in exchange for the said indebtedness at fifty per centum of said indebtedness, which bonds shall run for twenty years and bear interest at four per centum per annum. And said town authorities shall pay the floating debt of said town in full before the provisions of this act allowing an abrogation of the charter shall be of force.*

The act went on for eight more sections, stipulating the rules of debt repayment and explaining the repeal of the Fayetteville city charter. The years that Fayetteville essentially did not exist as a North Carolina city are known as the "Silent Years" because no town government of any type existed. Two years later, in 1883, the legislature awarded Fayetteville a restricted charter. The temporary charter existed for ten years to ensure that the city could live within its means, stipulating that the total annual expense of the city was limited to $3,000. Also under this arrangement, the town could elect boards of commissioners. They were authorized to levy a tax against town property owners and to collect privileges or license taxes. A "Taxing and Police District" was set up, and the town was able to resume enforcing these regulations. After a successful decade, the General Assembly of North Carolina met in 1893 and passed an act authorizing the reestablishment and reorganization of the city.

In May, city elections were held. W.S. Cook was elected mayor, and he hired fourteen prominent men as aldermen. Cook's first item on his agenda was to fix salaries for city officials. Salaries were set at $300 a year for the mayor, $600 a year for the chief of police, $500 for the assistant chief of police, $120 for clerk of court and $225 for the city treasurer. Cook also appointed chairmen for the following committees: police, printing and laws and ordinances. His main goal was to maintain Fayetteville's upward progress and to bring the city back from the brink of extinction. He was successful.

FAYETTEVILLE RAILROADS

Interestingly enough, Fayetteville claims to have had one of the first railroads in the United States. As Oates explains:

> *This road was built in 1828 and ran from the river up Bridge and Person Streets to the Market House. This was an experimental railroad to demonstrate to the people of the State the practicality of railroads. Major Hale said: "The road was constructed; but the wooden rails were convex at the top, the running surface of the wheels concave, the friction was too great and the experiment was not successful." But the significance of this date showing the enterprise of our people in those early days will be appreciated.*

It took until the late 1800s for Fayetteville to truly begin seeing the advent of railroads. In 1878, the first and only company, the Fayetteville & Western (F&W) Railroad, ran from the Cape Fear River to Jonesboro and then through Egypt, North Carolina—a total distance of fifty miles. The railroad's main purpose was to transport coal from mines to the Cape Fear River so that it would be transported down the river to oceangoing steamers.

This track saw one train a day going in either direction. The first left Fayetteville at 7:00 a.m., arriving in Egypt at 11:00 a.m. and then returning to Fayetteville by 3:30 p.m. The F&W Railroad established a lengthy list of taxable items, compiling these fees on a "Rates of Way—Freight and Passage" chart. For example, if traveling between Fayetteville and Wilmington, bringing an anvil cost twenty-five cents. Other fees were twenty-five cents per one hundred pounds of bacon, one dollar per bale of cotton, four dollars per cow, ten dollars for pianos and the most expensive: fifteen dollars for a pair of millstones. The list is very long and includes any- and everything one could imagine traveling with.

Even though the Fayetteville & Western was the only railroad company in Fayetteville, there were other tracks that ran through the city. For example, the Wilmington & Weldon ran to the east, the North Carolina Railroad to the north, the Raleigh & August to the west and the Carolina Central to the south.

Perhaps the most important of these tracks was the Wilmington & Weldon. A public law of 1893 authorized the commissioners of Fayetteville to enter into an agreement with the Wilmington & Weldon to build a passenger station on Hillsboro Street. The Wilmington & Weldon later became the Atlantic Coast Line.

Information given by the Atlantic Coast Line Railroad itself reads:

The route of the Atlantic Coast Line in the [18]80s was from Richmond to Wilmington; thence to Florence and Charleston, South Carolina. The through traffic from the north to the south was by Wilmington. In 1885 the Wilmington and Weldon Railroad began the construction of what was called the "Fayetteville Cut-off," from Wilson to Fayetteville and thence later to Pee Dee to tap the Wilmington, Columbia, and Augusta. This new line materially shortened the distance and running time and soon became the main line of the Atlantic Coast Line, and later double tracked from Richmond south, to Jacksonville, Florida.

About the turn of the century, several State Legislatures took the necessary action to permit the formation of the Atlantic Coast Line Railroad Company. These consolidated railroads pushed farther south...From Fayetteville, the Coast Line owns by purchase from the Old Cape Fear and Yadkin Valley Railroad, the lines to Wilmington, Bennettsville and Sanford...

All the through trains from Boston, New York and Philadelphia to Florida, over the Coast Line, pass through Fayetteville and the long fruit and vegetable trains from Florida, Georgia and South Carolina moving northward in season, pass through Fayetteville...Fayetteville is most fortunate in having one of the great southern railroads as its main transportation outlet.

QUIRKY MUSINGS WORTHY OF NOTE

In the 1870s, a very prominent young lawyer lived in Fayetteville (though there is no record of his name). It is said that he was bright, smart and ambitious—a great representation of the Fayetteville way of life. Because of this, he was invited to give a speech at the city's July Fourth celebration. He wrote his speech in full and gave it to a friend to edit and provide criticism.

On the day of the event, this friend was summoned to introduce the lawyer. Apparently, this friend had a memory as sharp as a tack and proceeded to give the lawyer's speech in full to the crowd. The crowd obviously thought that this speech was just part of the day's festivities, and as the friend finished, crowd members eagerly awaited the lawyer's speech.

When the lawyer was called to the stage, he floundered for a bit before trying to pull a new speech out of thin air. He said, "My fellow citizens, where we stand today, the Indians roamed and hunted two hundred years ago." He paused and apparently decided to start over.

This time he said, "My fellow citizens, where we stand today, the Indians roamed and hunted." He paused again and then in embarrassment quickly said, "And I wish they were here now." He jumped from the platform and left the festivities. There is no record whether the two men remained friends.

Another humorous story of the law involves prominent Fayetteville citizen Colonel C.W. Broadfoot. Colonel Broadfoot lived at the top of Haymount Hill, and in 1897, one of his cattle broke free from his property and proceeded to wander down the hill and into city limits. Technically, Colonel Broadfoot lived one mile from the town boundaries. A law had been passed in 1895 setting up a series of charges and penalties for cattle running at large in the city. When Broadfoot's cow was found roaming the streets alone, it was essentially arrested and taken to what was called the Cow Pound.

If a cow was arrested, residents of Fayetteville were required to pay one dollar, and those living within a mile of city limits had to pay a quarter of the charge (twenty-five cents). Colonel Broadfoot paid the twenty-five cents and expected to be on his way. The city refused to accept the twenty-five cents, stating that he had to pay the one-dollar fee. Because his home was exactly one mile from city limits, arguments arose over whether Broadfoot's property was part of the town or just outside it; this distinction affected how much he was supposed to pay for his cow.

Colonel Broadfoot, ever the stickler (but more an ardent believer in justice), took his case to court. He won. The city appealed the court's decision. Broadfoot won again. After all court cases were said and done, attorney fees on both sides of the case amounted to well above even the value of the cow. The city finally accepted the twenty-five cents for the cow.

The African American Way of Life

From the moment the war was over, black citizens began creating new opportunities for themselves.

Education was at the forefront of everyone's mind at the end of the Civil War, especially Fayetteville's African American population. Just a year after the war, a primary school was opened and was called the Phillips School. Sumner School, for intermediate education, was also opened. The schools operated separately for four years with the main goal of educating black youth. They were consolidated in 1869 and called the Howard School. The school assumed this name in honor of the Freedmen's Bureau chief, General O.O. Howard.

Seven prominent Fayetteville businessmen pooled together $136 in order to buy two lots along Gillespie Street for the first building that housed the Howard School. The men were Andrew J. Chesnutt, Thomas Lomax, George W. Granger Sr., Matthew N. Leary Jr., Robert H. Simmons, Nelson Carter and David Bryant, and they all became trustees of the school. The school's focus was to expound on what was already being taught at the Phillips School. Classes such as reading, writing and arithmetic and practical

The entire student body of the State Colored Normal School posed for this circa 1914 image outside of Aycock Hall (left) and Vance Hall (right). *Courtesy of Larry Tew.*

skills were offered in order to prepare the students to become teachers. The first principal of the Howard School was Robert Harris, and his main goal and focus was training teachers. Not only were his students trained to teach at the Howard School, but also they were certified to teach in small rural schools throughout Cumberland County.

Even during the economic recession spurred on by Reconstruction, the school was able to bring in donations. These donations were used to better the classrooms, purchase new equipment and employ teachers. The school was able to purchase a telescope and begin teaching science classes through these donations.

In 1877, the state legislature approved an act calling for the establishment of a teacher-training institution for African Americans. The Howard School was selected to be that institution. It assumed the name of the State Colored Normal School, thus becoming the first and oldest state-supported institution of its kind in North Carolina. A move to Murchison Road was made in 1907, and the fifty-acre stretch of land would remain the school's permanent location. The school operated until 1939, when it was renamed Fayetteville State Teachers College. Two more name changes (to Fayetteville State College in 1963 and Fayetteville State University in 1969) occurred before its last name change in the early 1970s.

In 1972, Fayetteville State University was made a constituent institution of the University of North Carolina, the oldest state-operated university in the country. This distinction solidified Fayetteville State University's role as North Carolina's second-oldest state education institution.

HOSPITALS

Before the war, Fayetteville was somewhat of a medical center for the South. Starting with Joseph Howard, a common doctor, and Thomas McDaniel Reed, a surgeon, the two worked the Cross Creek area from 1760 until the turn of the century. In 1805, Dr. Ben Robinson practiced medicine for more than fifty years, as did his son (called Young Dr. Ben for most of his life). Dr. Robinson's account book is housed at the Duke University archives and shows that a typical day was spent on house calls, sprinkled with the occasional birth (for which he charged a fee of fifteen dollars).

Dr. Robinson was instrumental in forming the Board of Health for Fayetteville, established in 1832 with the intention of developing ways to prevent the spread of cholera and other epidemics. Dr. Robinson worked with the Board of Health until his death in 1857. At that time, a study was done on the life span of Fayetteville citizens. Public records show that 102 people died in Fayetteville in 1857; most lived until at least the age of 50, with one citizen living until the age of 102.

St. Luke's Hospital was built in 1904 by Dr. John Henry Marsh. The building was quite impressive and was unlike anything in town at the time. Built at the top of the Haymount Hill (simply called "the Hill" by locals) at the crossroads of Morganton Road, Broadfoot and Highland Streets and Arsenal Avenue, the design of the hospital was an excellent example of premodern structures.

At the start of his practice, Dr. Marsh opened a nurse-training program in town, employing the nurses at his hospital. They wore long white dresses with aprons and white hats.

The hospital had a tall tower sticking straight up from its roof. This was considered to be a breakthrough for care of patients with respiratory ailments; those who had trouble breathing were housed in the top of the tower with the idea that getting them as far up into clean air as possible was best for their sickness.

This 1910 image of St. Luke's Hospital clearly shows the tower that housed patients with respiratory ailments. *Courtesy of the North Carolina State Archives.*

This image shows the Haymount residential area, named in the 1780s by John Hay. Some of the houses in this area boast architectural nuances from St. Luke's Hospital. *Courtesy of Larry Tew.*

Doctors T. Marshall West and R.B. Hayes joined Dr. Marsh at St. Luke's Hospital and worked with him for several years. When Dr. Marsh died in 1910, the property was sold, and St. Luke's was demolished. Elements that were salvaged from St. Luke's (mainly columns and dormers) were used in building a number of houses in Haymount. Many of the houses on Broadfoot Street and Arsenal Avenue still maintain these design elements.

Dr. West and Dr. Hayes then went on to establish the Fayetteville Infirmary in 1912. The building, an imposing brick structure, was built closer to downtown and later changed its name to Cumberland General Hospital. Finally, the hospital closed in 1926 and was turned into a hotel, the Ivy Inn.

Dr. Jacob Franklin Highsmith was also a prominent healthcare provider in town. He had the first modern hospital built in town in 1906 after a fire destroyed the 1896 sanitarium that stood on the same spot. The Highsmith Hospital was located downtown on Green Street, taking up most of the block that started at Market Square and continued down to Old Street. In 1926, Highsmith Hospital was relocated to the corner of Hay and Bradford Streets, where it still stands today, serving as the Cumberland County Mental Health Center.

INDUSTRY

The few mills that existed in Fayetteville in the mid-1800s were small, water-powered factories in Hope Mills, Manchester and Fayetteville. It was these mills that cemented Fayetteville's role in antebellum textile manufacturing. They were all victims of Sherman's torch, leaving Fayetteville to start over almost entirely after the war. The only mill that was left standing was the Beaver Creek Mill in Rockfish (later Hope Mills). Rumor has it that the mill was only spared because its superintendent was a native of the same Massachusetts town as the Union troop assigned to burn it down.

Ever resilient, Fayetteville soon bounced back. Never again would it be the top of industry as it once had been, but textile manufacturing was still a vital part of the economy. Soon, mills were becoming joint ventures, benefiting several families in the Fayetteville area. As Roy Parker wrote in *Cumberland County: A Brief History*:

> *While the earlier factories were launched and financed largely by local enterprise, the postwar additions often resulted from joint enterprise of noted*

state textile barons, particularly the Holt family of Alamance County, in alliance with professional textile operatives and local investors.

In 1898, the Holt-Morgan plant was built in Massey Hill (a small working district adjacent to downtown Fayetteville). The plant was state-of-the-art, with ten thousand spindles. Two years later, just past Holt-Morgan, another plant opened. The "Happy Village of Tolar-Hart" was a two-story factory built on 190 acres. Containing small cottages for workers to live in, the factory became somewhat of a model for family-owned industrial operations.

The "Happy Village" (as it was called in advertising) had everything a family could want: a small library, a community hall, an Episcopal chapel, a playground, a baseball field and tennis court. Owner John Tolar hired two full-time village employees (Ollie Vick Livingstone and Lucy Currie). They were hired to teach night school and kindergarten, organize clubs, run the library and build community spirit.

Children pose outside of Tolar-Hart. The plant depended on the child workforce until child labor laws were enforced. *Library of Congress Prints & Photographs Division.*

Parker continued describing the factory, writing that

> *despite the paternal atmosphere, Tolar-Hart employees worked long hours for*
> *the low wages of the time. Families had from five to seven children, and*
> *most of them worked in the mill until the child labor laws were passed and*
> *enforced. One mill worker reported in 1896: "We have a public school here,*
> *but the factory people cannot spare their children from the mill to attend it.*
> *They are too poor. If they were to send them, it would be against the wishes*
> *of the managers to do so, as they need the children's labor in the mill." Pay*
> *rates were 58 to 83 cents a day for men and 40 to 75 cents a day for women.*

Ollie Livingstone kept a journal during her employment at Tolar-Hart. She described the workers' cottages, saying:

> *Most of the houses had three large rooms. The long kitchen had a table and a*
> *stove at opposite ends of the room. The bedrooms were off the main room. At*
> *least once a week, the pine floors were scrubbed with corn shucks and lye soap.*
> *Each house had its own garden and most families had some pigs and chickens.*

The cottages were owned by Tolar-Hart until after World War II.

Even greater than Tolar-Hart's success was that of the Ashley-Bailey Silk Company, Fayetteville's most noteworthy textile enterprise. The company's two three-story brick structures were built in 1900 on Robeson Street, one mile from Tolar-Hart. Ashley-Bailey was unique in that it employed only black workers—and mainly women at that—the total opposite of the typical textile workforce. In 1914, the factory reported having twenty-six thousand spindles and 472 looms, which processed 135 tons of raw silk a year and produced $375,000 annually.

There were 310 female and 135 male workers. Wages ranged from sixty-five cents to three dollars for a ten-hour day. An extensive factory village sprang up around the factory, called Ashley Heights. The streets were named after silk-making processes, like Italy, German and Belgium. The area is still inhabited, though the mill closed years ago, leaving the two main buildings for use today by other businesses. It is still called Ashley Heights.

Later, the company acquired hundreds of acres of piney forest and ponds that were adjacent to the factory site. These grounds now house Highland Country Club and residential neighborhoods.

The Ashley-Bailey Silk Mill opened and revolutionized the textile industry in Fayetteville circa 1910. *Courtesy of the North Carolina State Archives.*

By 1916, Fayetteville's business directory boasted more than three hundred businesses, including four bicycle shops, three five-and-ten-cent stores, two florists and a Chinese laundry called Wah Sing. There were three banks and two savings and loans, nineteen firms selling insurance, six hotels, nine inns and classical trades such as five carriage dealers and eight horse and mule dealers. Automobiles were becoming more and more popular, so Fayetteville also contained three "garages."

By the turn of the century, Fayetteville manufacturing had changed drastically from the cart-and-buggy industries of postwar America. Candy makers, beer distillers, brick makers, bakers, druggists—you name it. Fayetteville had it all, and people were buying it, setting Fayetteville up for an incredibly successful twentieth century.

VII

A NEW CENTURY, A NEW LEGACY

At the turn of the century, Fayetteville had beaten the recession spurred on by the end of the Civil War. Its industries were booming, families were thriving and new municipal buildings like courthouses were in constant construction.

Fayetteville even saw its first automobile in 1902 (the owner claimed it was even the first car in the state of North Carolina). The city's first "gasoline car" drove down Hay Street creating quite a stir. Citizens called it a buggy or a horseless carriage, complaining that it "tore through the city" at a whopping ten miles per hour.

To accompany the distinction of having the first automobile, Fayetteville also boasts another first that is incredibly noteworthy. In the early 1900s, baseball was very popular, quickly becoming America's favorite pastime. In March 1914, the Baltimore Orioles held spring training in Fayetteville, bringing with them relative newcomer George Herman "Babe" Ruth.

In town for a month, Ruth later wrote about his time in Fayetteville, as it was his first time ever leaving the city of Baltimore. He wrote about how much fun he had riding the elevators in his hotel. While in town, the young Ruth didn't know what to do out on his own. Rumor has it that he constantly tagged along with Orioles manager and owner Jack Dunn, causing one of his teammates to quip, "There goes Dunn's new babe." The nickname stuck.

On March 7, 1914, Ruth played in his first Orioles game. He hit a long home run. It was estimated that the ball traveled 350 feet in the air, sailed

Above: Men of Fayetteville stand in front of the Old Courthouse at its location in St. James Square in this early 1900–10 depiction. *Courtesy of the North Carolina State Archives.*

Left: "Babe" Ruth plays baseball in Fayetteville with his team, the Baltimore Orioles, in 1914. *Library of Congress Prints & Photographs Division.*

over the park fence and landed in a cornfield. Not only was it the longest hit any of the spectators had seen, but it was also Ruth's first professional home run. He later commented, "I hit as I hit all the others, by taking a good gander at the pitch as it came up to the plate, twisting my body into a backswing, and then hitting it as hard as I could swing."

His nickname was cemented during this first home run, when it is said that one of his teammates whistled and said under his breath, "Look at that babe go!" Just as Ruth never forgot his visit to Fayetteville, Fayetteville never forgot Ruth or the career-changing events that happened on its soil.

FLOODS

On August 25, 1908, Fayetteville experienced one of the worst floods in its history. Waters rose all the way up to the block of the Town House, causing Cross Creek to become a torrent on Person and Green Streets. For days, families had to get around town in small punts (boats used for creek fishing). There were a few attempts made to travel by horse and buggy, though they were premature. Horses were getting stuck in deep puddles, and wheels were becoming clogged with mud and debris.

Many of the homes on Green and Person Streets had to be evacuated. Because waters from the Cape Fear River and Cross Creek converged at those points, the homes located on those streets fared the worst. Quite a few residents had to use their boats to search for people who were trapped inside their homes. Floodwaters remained until September 1, when they finally started to recede and people were able to begin cleanup.

However, the city's worst flood came in 1945. The Cape Fear River rose to its highest level ever recorded, some two feet higher than the 1908 flood. As Oates recalls:

> *The river gauge at the Clarendon Bridge was 68.9 feet...the flood waters were more than four miles wide at Fayetteville. Hundreds of families were evacuated in Fayetteville and across the river from the city. One life was lost—a man who went into the flood waters to get his cow and was drowned.*

In an anniversary newspaper article, a Mrs. C.H. Coats was quoted describing the events as she saw them:

This postcard shows the downtown area during the flood of 1908. Waters began to recede, but horses and carriages still got stuck in the mud. *Courtesy of Larry Tew.*

"Everybody was in a jitter. I will never forget it. It wasn't a nice place to be. Everybody was trying to conserve [for the war effort], *had chickens and raising gardens.*

I had some chickens—they were just beautiful. I had to go out to the chicken coop and sit them on a higher place where they wouldn't drown. The water had come up so quickly. A transformer blew up, I guess. Person Street lit up like I'd never seen it before. I'd never seen anything so pretty. It was breathtaking to see all that fire falling in the water."

The rising waters still threatened the chickens, so Mrs. Coats contracted a boat ($5 or $10 she recalls) to take the chickens and her toddling son, Max, to Liberty Point, where her sister would meet her.

"You could walk out, I'm five-nine, and it was up to my shoulders. There was this nice looking soldier across the street, all stiff in his uniform, and he asked 'could I please ride in your boat, I've got to get to Fort Bragg.' It wasn't very long before we hit a fire hydrant and the boat turned over. The man we had in uniform was so stiff and pretty, he just melted. I had on a gingham dress and it started to shrink. It turned into a bathing suit. And you know back then, a woman didn't appear on the street in a bathing suit, so I stayed in the water. We gathered up the chickens that were still alive and I gave them to my sister."

"I had to walk back to the house and the water was up to my chin. I had to hold Max, 2 or 3 at the time, up over my head. We were without water and lights for weeks. The damage was terrific, and you know back then, insurance didn't pay for a thing. But my house was high, and we didn't get the damage that a lot of them did."

Several precautions had to be taken to ensure that townspeople did not become ill. Houses were evacuated and their residents vaccinated against malaria by army medical officers as they removed from flood zones. The army sent five hundred gallons of DDT to forestall a possible epidemic of malaria and typhoid, as all the standing water was a hotbed for mosquitoes and other bugs.

A second newspaper article described in detail all the steps residents had to take to ensure their safety upon reinhabiting their homes:

Four ounces of chlorine powder will be distributed to every family before they return home together with a list of instructions outlining its use. The proper proportions are one level tablespoons of chlorine to 5 gallons of water and this preparation should be used for both scrubbing and as a disinfectant. [It is] urged that everything possible be boiled. Those items which it is impossible to boil should be thoroughly washed and then sprayed with the chlorine solution. This should include absolutely everything that has been contaminated by the flood waters, clothing, bedding, furniture, etc...

In addition, all water used except city water should be boiled for five minutes. It is the plan of the health department to visit all of the inundated houses as soon as the water recedes.

Water began receding after nearly a week, and life was able to carry on as normal.

THE CLARENDON BRIDGE

During the Civil War, the Clarendon Bridge was of great interest to General Sherman and his armies, as it was the easiest way to cross the Cape Fear River. At that time, it was a covered wooden bridge. There is a legend in

Fayetteville that during the construction of the wooden bridge, the roof was covered in shingles, and one of the men working on the roof slipped. He was undoubtedly frightened, as the drop to the water was more than fifty feet. As he slid to the edge, the seat of his pants caught on a nail and held him until he was rescued. As the story in Oates's book goes, the man "thought so much of the nail that saved his life that he took it out, had it plated with gold and kept it."

In March 1865, the bridge was burned by Confederate troops to thwart Sherman's advances. Sherman had two pontoon bridges constructed, one of which resumed the name of Clarendon Bridge (despite the fact that it was in a different location; records vary on whether it was two, three or four miles away from the original spot).

The flood of 1908 damaged the bridge; the water pressure caused it to bend out of line.

Shortly after the flood, in February 1909, the bridge was completely destroyed again. A local farmer named Britt was burning a cornfield on the western side of the bridge. There is a rumor floating around Fayetteville that residents did not care for the bridge in the first place, maybe because Sherman built it or maybe because it was unsightly, no one really knows. So when Britt's fire destroyed the bridge, residents were actually thrilled,

Townspeople stand back and watch as the Clarendon Bridge burns, February 3, 1909. *Courtesy of the North Carolina State Archives.*

and he was rewarded by being named police chief—a distinction that must have been quite important at the time, though it now requires a bit more know-how.

In July 1909, a new steel structure was constructed; it was used until 1937. In that year, yet another bridge was constructed right next to the old bridge. It adopted the name Soldiers and Sailors of World War Bridge. This is the structure that still stands today, crossing over Person Street.

WORLD WAR I

The United States entered World War I on April 6, 1917, employing Cumberland County citizens answering their nation's call. Under the Selective Service Act, 3,379 county men were registered with the army. At the end of April, the first draft quota was met with 222 men from Cumberland County. They were trained and sent off (most in the 80th Division, the 92nd and the Air Service). The Fayetteville Independent Light Infantry was also called to arms. It was registered as Company F of the 119th Infantry Regiment, part of the 30th Division fighting in Flanders, Belgium.

War efforts at home were lively and aggressive. Roy Parker wrote:

> *Civilians participated in Liberty Bond drives—the county's quota in the fourth drive was $780,000, an amount equal to twice the taxes paid to the county government in 1917. They joined the Red Cross to wrap bandages and prepare gift boxes for soldiers. They gathered at the railroad station to cheer as groups of draftees and National Guard units boarded for training camps.*

As it is with every war, loss is inevitable. Cumberland County's first loss was Private Cyrus Adcox, a twenty-year-old who hailed from a family in the Holt-Morgan textile factory neighborhood in Massey Hill. He was killed in action on May 29, 1918, serving with the machine gun battalion of the Thirtieth Division. A memorial service was held for him at Holt-Morgan; hymns were sung by the choir from the neighboring (and competing) Tolar-Hart factory community.

Men fought until Armistice on November 11, 1918. Scores of decorated soldiers began flooding their hometown of Fayetteville. Private Edward

Draughton of the sanitary detachment of the 30th Division won the Distinguished Service Cross for bravery in action. First Lieutenant Daniel Byrd of Company F, 119th Infantry (mostly composed of Cumberland County men), won the same. Possibly most notable was Captain Donald Ray. A Fayetteville man, he worked as a lawyer on the staff of the chief of artillery in Washington, D.C. He made it his goal to acquire Fayetteville as the site for an artillery range and training camp, action that would change the destiny of Fayetteville forever.

FORT BRAGG

Washington, D.C.'s chief of artillery was Colonel E.P. King. One humid day in June 1918, King traveled down to Fayetteville at the request of Captain Ray. Accompanied by Dr. T. Wayland Vaughn of the United States Geological Survey, the two men were under assignment to survey a parcel of land for an artillery range and camp. As Roy Parker recalls:

> *On the evening of their fourth day from Washington,* [the two men] *topped a rise just beyond the crossroads of Manchester on the Lower Little River. King later recalled that as he and Vaughn looked out across the undulating, pine-covered sand ridges, they knew they had found the site they had been searching for.*

The War Department, headed by Major General William J. Snow, later announced that Camp Bragg (named for Civil War Confederate general Braxton Bragg) would find its home in 133,760 acres of the rolling sand hills of Fayetteville, North Carolina.

Corps of ditch diggers and carpenters flooded the area, starting work on carving roads, construction of wooden buildings and designing water-flow and sewer systems. A booklet called *Camp Bragg and Fayetteville: Sketches of a Camp and City* recalls the relationships between construction workers as being very good, providing a positive, productive work environment. The booklet reads:

> *For the most part, the character of the men was the best to be found anywhere upon the American continent. A large percentage came from*

The pine tree–laden land the War Department had been looking for was found in an area called Overhills, about eight miles from the city center of Fayetteville. *Library of Congress Prints & Photographs Division.*

nearby farms and small localities in North Carolina and contiguous states. Many a farmer left his home after harvest and passed the winter in profitable endeavor. A large number also came from the great labor centers of the north, and there were found to be enterprising and moral. They were for the most part men desirous of spending a delightful winter away from the scenes of vice and lawlessness, with the attendant opportunities for saving the greater part of their earnings. The isolation of the camp ten miles from the nearest town, Fayetteville, enabled comparatively easy enforcement of the prohibition law and there was as a consequence, a minimum of violence and crime. No agitation occurred to mar the peaceful pursuit of the work. This is a remarkable record when the paucity of the military and the almost entire absence of civil authority is considered in the control of a somewhat heterogeneous force of over seven thousand men. There were no tragedies.

This "Greetings From Fort Bragg, N.C." postcard depicts four major military buildings: the Air Corps Barracks at Pope Field, Post Headquarters, the Station Hospital and the Thirty-sixth Field Artillery Barracks. *Courtesy of Larry Tew.*

Because the workers got on so amiably, base construction went exceedingly fast and took just under a year, with work being completed in the spring of 1919. At that time, the camp could hold almost twenty thousand soldiers.

In the northern corner of the camp, an airfield was laid down in order to accommodate the popular "Flying Jenny" airplanes of the time. In January 1919, Lieutenant Harley Pope was flying with his friend Sergeant W.W. Fleming. Their plane crashed into the Cape Fear River, killing them both. This stretch of airfield was named Pope Field to honor the pilot; this would later become Pope Air Force Base (and now Pope Army Airfield).

Even though World War I ended before the completion of Camp Bragg, it was still retained by the army to house permanent artillery units. Until 1920, twelve hundred troops were stationed at Camp Bragg. Not foreseeing any upcoming military conflicts, the War Department announced in the summer of 1921 that Camp Bragg would be abandoned. The camp commander, Colonel Albert Bowley, did not approve of this decision and took it upon himself to change it. After bringing several important people to town (including the secretary of war), the ruling was reversed. It's a good thing it was because Camp Bragg would become the largest military installation in the United States and one of the most active bases in the entire world.

Parker writes:

Bowley remained commander of the camp he had saved until 1929. By then, the name had been changed to Fort Bragg and a 1923–1928 building program had replaced many of the cantonment's original wooden structures with permanent brick buildings. Pope Field got a large hangar for its observation balloons. As early as July 4, 1923, soldiers were parachuting from balloon platforms, a harbinger of Fort Bragg's future role as "Home of the Airborne." Additional construction in the 1930s created an installation of about 3,000 soldiers and 350 civilian workers. From the start, the post contributed significantly to the Cumberland economy. It spawned a fleet of "jitney" taxicabs linking the camp with the railroad depot in Fayetteville. Dozens of civilians became permanent employees in post laundries, kitchens, warehouses, offices, and public works.

SOLDIERS' COMPASSION

In Fort Bragg's early days, an old ex-slave named John Nichols was found to be living on the military reservation. His home had been there since the end of the Civil War, and he refused to leave, despite the fact that his home was in the middle of the long-range-shooting practice field. The newspaper did a story on Mr. Nichols. It read:

The farmers and tenants of the reservation gathered together all their pigs, chickens, horses, and household belongings and departed; only John Nichols remained.

Army rangers reported to General Bowley that John Nichols had refused to obey his order for all civilians to leave the reservation, and that he still lived in his tumble down hut, feeding his pigs and tapping pine trees for turpentine. The General sent a hard-boiled Army sergeant out to move the Negro off the reservation.

The sergeant and his detail loaded Nichols, his pigs, chickens, and his scanty belongings on a truck and carried them to the edge of the reservation and dumped them out. The next morning the rangers reported that the Negro was back at his cabin again with his pigs and his chickens.

The Army General detailed a captain and more men to put Nichols off the reservation. Again the pigs, chicken, and Nichols' belongings were gathered into an Army truck, and the whole outfit carried to the edge of the reservation and left. Next morning the fire in the old Negro's kitchen was again burning and he was back with all his belongings.

General Bowley phoned a Fayetteville lawyer and asked him if he would go out to the reservation that evening and tell John Nichols to get off.

The party drove out to the reservation where Nichols' log cabin was located. The [man] was sitting in the door of his humble shack with an open Bible in his lap. He laid his book down and took his hat, walked over to the car and said, "Good evening white folks."

"Nichols, I have brought a Judge out here to tell you that you must get off the reservation and stay off," said General Bowley.

[Nichols] stood and thought a while and then he said almost tearfully, "General, Sir, I can't do it."

He explained further that at the end of the Civil War he had promised a white family that he would stay and look after them. He kept his promise to stay on the farm of Mrs. Ray, cultivated the sand hill land and chipped the few pines that were left for turpentine and made tar from the lightwood knots. Nichols told them the angels told him when the firing was going to begin and he got out of the way. Finally the general said, "Well Negro, you stay right here."

Nichols was adopted by the Officers' Club. He was fed and cared for by the forest rangers. They took him to the Army hospital when it was evident that he would not live long, and he said to the doctors, "I'm going to die. Leave me at home." They carried him back to his cabin. The rangers furnished him with medicine and a nurse.

Nichols did not live long after that, though he remained eternally bonded to his word, a man of honor and good faith.

POPULATION

Starting about 1920, Fayetteville began seeing sharp spikes in its population, and these spikes were mainly attributed to Fort Bragg. Between 1920 and 1930, Fayetteville's population spiked 46 percent, growing from 8,887 to 13,039. It grew another almost 34 percent between 1930 and 1940 (from

13,039 to 17,428). Cumberland County saw the same figures. The county's population surged 70 percent between 1920 and 1940, growing from 35,064 to 59,320 people.

The influx of people was not always welcomed or appreciated. Some citizens of Fayetteville viewed the extreme rise in population as negative, especially considering the actions and attitudes of some of the Fort Bragg soldiers. Businesses were heavily infiltrated, with one magazine article citing Fayetteville as an "American community which is trying under the most unusual circumstances to do its best for soldiers, who outnumber its pre-boom civilian population more than four to one and who strain its every facility to the snapping point."

Because Fayetteville's population essentially doubled overnight without its resources changing a bit, the city ran into trouble accommodating everyone. As the *News and Observer* out of Raleigh stated, "And so enough new problems have come to this once quiet Southern city to leave the town fathers dizzy."

The biggest issue became housing. Every room in town was filled, be it boardinghouse, inn or hotel. Newspaper articles recount living conditions:

The inscription on this postcard reads, "Business Section, Looking East on Hay Street, Fayetteville, North Carolina," showing a busy workday in downtown. *Courtesy of Larry Tew.*

There can be no exaggeration of the desperate living conditions obtained here. There is no choice of rooms for a newcomer. Rents have been forced up, not only by acquisitive landlords but by room seekers outbidding each other.
…Many landlords openly state their preference for male tenants, who are "less bother," "don't want parlor privileges," and "are willing to double up on beds." Although rooms may be obtained for less than $30 a month, most of them at this price are pathetic pigeon holes, lacking comfortable chairs, closet space, rugs and any desirable standard of cleanliness.

The small answer to this problem was the Soldiers' Town Home. People of Fayetteville joined together to convert a deserted home on Old Street into a transitory home for soldiers passing through Fayetteville. A newspaper article described the home:

The forlorn erstwhile derelict building has comforted many a weary heart, has offered new courage to worn and foot sore travelers and consolation to mothers, wives and sweethearts of American fighting men…"I just didn't feel like I had really been home until I got here," Pfc. Bill Green said. He is resting after service in Africa and Sicily. That's typical of what the Town

This postcard image of the Soldiers' Town Home bestows on it the distinction of being the "original recreation home for soldiers." *Courtesy of Larry Tew.*

Home does for the boys; takes them in, mothers them, spoils them and sends them away with the assurance that the welcome mat will be spread on the door for them whenever they come back from whenever they go.

Over thirty thousand soldiers passed through the Soldiers' Town Home during its lifetime.

THE STOCK MARKET CRASHES

Of course, as soon as the United States recovers from one pitfall, it experiences another. Monday, October 28, 1929, was essentially a day just like any other. Fayetteville residents slept soundly in their beds, aware that problems existed on Wall Street but not realizing that the next day would bring a ten-year period of economic upheaval. The *Fayetteville Observer* ran an article the day before Black Tuesday titled "Stock Market is on the Toboggan as Prices Break," citing that

Wall Street was thrown into turmoil again today by another disastrous break in stock prices, which carried scores of issues down $5 to $45 a share, many of them below the low levels reached in last Thursday's record-breaking session...Today's break coming on the heels of a report that a powerful banking pool had been organized last week to support the market, caused consternation among thousands of speculators who had held on in the belief that the worst was over.

Surprisingly, the October 30 issue of the *Fayetteville Observer* contained no big headlines on the event. Two front-page stock market stories were overshadowed by headlines that an attorney was on trial for murder and a missing plane had been found in New Mexico. One of the columns was commentary compiled by the Associate Press, pulling excerpts from North Carolina newspapers that had commented on the crash.

The Durham newspaper simply quipped:

The shaking down of the stock market was but the natural result of the working of sound economic law. Many stocks under the speculative stimulus had built up excessive values and it was inevitable that the time would come

when circumstances would force a readjustment on a sounder basis. The present situation probably will result in a more conservative market for some months to come, and if it does, great sums of money will be released for other lines. The country's economic situation has not been seriously damaged. Fundamentally, business is as sound as it has been for some time.

The *Birmingham* [Alabama] *Age-Herald* wrote:

No thoughtful person can regard what has taken place as less than good and hopeful. The country had gone speculation mad. It is worthwhile for the sake of the larger good that even so drastic a liquidation as has been witnessed should have taken place. There will be no panic because the United States has gotten beyond that stage in its economic development and because resources are available through the Federal Reserve to prevent such a calamity.

Optimistic articles one day led to pessimistic articles another, as headlines changed daily from trumpeting rising prices to record sessions spurred by a "mad scramble" to buy stocks. Panic and despair eventually reigned when people truly began to realize the severity of the economy's state.

FARMING AND TEXTILES

With the stock market crash in 1929 and the subsequent onset of the Great Depression, residents of Fayetteville were living a hard life. Fayetteville's economy always mirrored that of the rest of the country, and this was no exception since the majority of the Fayetteville workforce was made up of farmers. Farmers witnessed catastrophic drops in crop prices. Cotton went from $150 a bale to $13 a bale (that is, if anyone was buying). Tobacco fell from forty-seven cents to eight cents a pound.

One of the greatest problems that farmers faced was the fact that more than half of them were sharecroppers who did not own the land they farmed. Crops, especially cotton, were in extreme overproduction, which was catastrophic when met with declining prices. Farmers were losing their livelihood. As North Carolina contained more famers than any other state besides Texas, this agricultural recession hit especially close to home. In

1929, North Carolina's gross farming income was $310.5 million, but by 1932 that number had dropped by more than half. By 1932, one in four was completely unemployed, while those county workers with jobs worked for months without pay because Cumberland County residents were unable to pay their taxes.

Somewhat of a domino effect ensued. As farm prices fell, banks began to close. Because the banks were closing, businesses were forced to shut their doors as a result of not being able to get credit. Farmers, trying to repay the loans on their equipment, began to borrow from savings and loans. When those businesses began to fail in 1932, more farms were foreclosed upon.

Citizens began withdrawing everything they had from county banks. In January 1932, two of Fayetteville's three banks were forced to shut their doors. The Caledonian Savings and Trust and the Cumberland National Bank both closed, Cumberland National for good.

For those residents who were able to maintain their jobs, mill owners forced their employees to work longer hours doing harder jobs in a last-ditch effort to remain competitive. The Victory Mill in Massey Hill paid out roughly $1.50 for a full week's work. Even those who could work were hopelessly poor.

The *Fayetteville Observer* ran an article in the 1950s titled "Prosperous County Had Ration Lines in '30s," written by Bobbie Brewer. It recounts some of the actions taken by city officials to pull Cumberland County out of this terrible depression, especially as the lack of money meant a severe lack of food. Brewer asked:

> *Remember the bleak days of the "depression"? The stark, lean years without work, many people without money and many starving. The years when a breadline was the "task" of the day and fatback, meal and molasses a Sunday feast?*

Residents of Fayetteville became angry at the lack of food and marched to the sheriff's office, demanding a change. A man by the name of Butler spoke, saying, "We are desperate and we are liable to do anything before we see our wives and little children starve to death. We need something to eat at once. Many of us have not even had as much as a mouthful of bread today."

Two city aldermen were able to arrange for food. Rations were established for families of varying sizes, giving fifteen pounds of meal, three pounds of meat, two pounds of lard, a quart of syrup and four pounds of peas for a family of five.

Possibly the saddest of days arrived before Christmas 1932, when the *Fayetteville Observer* had to make a plea for donations. The paper printed:

> *Hundreds of little children in this city are counting on being present at a Christmas tree Christmas Eve. They will not hang stockings that night because they have learned to their sorrow that Santa Claus does not come to houses occupied by poor people.*

In an attempt to make life in Fayetteville a little bit easier, an act of the legislature authorized Cumberland County to begin paying its employees in scrip pay. Additionally, volunteer programs began popping up in the city, like the Parent-Teachers Association free-lunch program and the "Emergency Relief Canteen."

With President Roosevelt's election and subsequent New Deal plan, the city began to slowly pull itself out of its rut. Projects financed by the Emergency Relief Act and the Civil Works Act brought jobs to town, totaling in excess of $300,000 in 1934 and '35. Roy Parker wrote of these projects, saying that

> *the largest of these was a $100,000 home sanitation project involving construction and installation of hundreds of wooden privies.* [As late as 1940, only one in thirty farm homes in Cumberland County had indoor plumbing, and only one in nine had electricity.] *Several miles of mosquito-control drainage ditches were dug in Fayetteville, Cedar Creek, Hope Mills, Flea Hill, and Wade. Roads were repaired, as were schools...Fayetteville Normal School got a playing field, a new road, and repairs—projects totaling $15,000. Salaries were provided for playground supervisors, cooks, nurses, secretaries, school lunchroom supervisors, workers for a "sewing room" program.*

No matter the job, Fayetteville residents were just happy to finally be working again. In 1936, cotton prices began to creep up. Costs had reached $62 a bale (a far cry from before the panic but certainly better than just after). Tobacco began to draw twenty-four cents a pound just as the New Deal price support program gained steam. In 1938, tobacco was the top money crop in Cumberland County, bringing in $905,000.

Parker provides interesting workforce statistics during the Great Depression:

Not until 1940 did employment recover to pre-Depression levels. In that year, 20,000 people were wage earners—4,700 on farms, 3,500 in manufacturing, 10,300 in retailing and construction, and 1,500 on the expanding Fort Bragg payroll. In 1930, by comparison, there had been 6,000 paid workers on farms, 3,800 in manufacturing, and 7,800 in other jobs. Value added by manufacture, $2.7 million in pre-Depression 1927, was almost exactly the same in 1939.

A VISIT FROM THE FIRST LADY

In 1912, Fayetteville received permission to construct a rail depot on Hillsboro Street to be connected to the Atlantic Coast Line, thereby connecting Fayetteville to virtually every major city on the eastern seaboard. The depot has seen many important people throughout the years, including the wife of President Franklin D. Roosevelt.

In 1934, First Lady Eleanor Roosevelt paid an unexpected visit to Fayetteville. She was on a train en route to Florida from Washington, and her train stopped ever so briefly at the Fayetteville depot, giving the first lady a chance to stretch her legs. On the streets of downtown for only twelve minutes, she made the most of her short visit, expressing interest in the city's history and wanting to get a look at the Town House.

Fayetteville Observer reporter R.L. Gray Jr. had the opportunity to escort Mrs. Roosevelt through the town, answering her questions and providing her with pamphlets and booklets. He wrote an article for the paper on March 5, 1934, saying:

We walked down the south side of Hay Street and it was amusing to see the people's mouths hang open when they recognized Mrs. Roosevelt.

At the Methodist Church corner, Mrs. Roosevelt decided to forego the enjoyment of viewing the Market House from closer range and stepped out into the street to see it…

We started back with Mrs. Roosevelt still displaying an avid interest in the history of Fayetteville. I ran ahead then to the Chamber of Commerce where I found Col. H.C. Pond had anticipated Mrs. Roosevelt's wishes and armed himself with a sheath of pamphlets, booklets, and other information which he presented to Mrs. Roosevelt as she passed.

Mr. Gray was also bold enough to comment on the first lady's appearance, writing, "Mrs. Roosevelt was dressed in a lightweight dark blue suit with a white blouse and a large white collar. She was hatless. She is much better looking than her photographs."

The Veterans' Hospital

In 1938, the Veterans' Administration considered building a hospital in eastern North Carolina. Fayetteville citizens heard of this announcement and decided to select a committee to work toward securing Fayetteville as the hospital's location. Thomas Hunter was elected chairman, and he selected a committee of businessmen.

Through their hard work, Fayetteville was selected to be the location for the new Veterans' Administration Hospital. Ground was broken on May 17, 1939. The building was completed and dedicated on October 17, 1940.

The Veterans' Administration Hospital, which opened on Ramsey Street in 1940, contains a replica of the Town House in its central tower. *Courtesy of Larry Tew.*

The architects who designed the building borrowed the same motif as the Town House and even carved a replica of it in the hospital's front façade. Upon completion, the hospital was called the finest, most modern and best-kept hospital in the country, boasting 416 beds, forty-six physicians and surgeons, twenty-two dentists, three chiropractors, three optometrists and one chiropodist.

During construction, crumbled walls and old stones were found on the property. Historians were able to surmise that these were breastworks built during the Civil War. As the study reads, "The old Breastworks ran across the Road to the east toward the Cape Fear River, and to the west to the Rose Hill Road on the hill of Cross Creek."

Oates commented:

> Breastworks were thrown up early in 1865 about the time that General Sherman reached Columbia on his march north. It was thought that he might swing around and come into Fayetteville from the north. The Breastworks were never used.

Despite the fact that they were not used, the Confederate breastworks remained standing as a testament to the Civil War era. The breastworks have been preserved on the property of the Veterans' Administration Hospital and are visible today.

The end of the 1930s brought more stirrings of war and European conflict. When Fayetteville was celebrating the 200th anniversary of its settlement, the city and Fort Bragg began to arm themselves, bracing for upheaval.

VIII

FAYETTEVILLE AND THE SECOND WORLD WAR

M any events could be credited with spawning the Second World War, but the event that brought the most destruction, the one that called for the most arms and assistance, was the blitzkrieg attack on Poland by the Germans on September 1, 1939. This "Lightning War" happened so fast that Poland's air force was destroyed while still on the ground. That same day, Great Britain and France sent Hitler an ultimatum: he should withdraw all of his forces from Poland or Great Britain and France would go to war against Germany.

Of course, Hitler would agree to no such ultimatum. On September 3, as German troops bled deeper and deeper into Poland, Great Britain and France declared war on Germany. World War II had begun.

MOBILIZATION OF FORT BRAGG

With conflict in Europe escalating by the day, Fort Bragg began to expand the army, preparing for playing a major part in the war effort. In August 1940, Fort Bragg's accolades grew almost as fast as Fayetteville's population. The fort became the sole training location of the Ninth Infantry Division, a major hub of artillery replacement and the location for many new engineer and service units, as well as a rallying point for draftees (both local and out-of-state).

Many prominent Fayetteville names served on the selective service board for the draft in Fayetteville. For example, members included Charles Rose Sr., Thomas Rankin, J. Warren Pate and Gilbert Martin. The government appeal agents were none other than Mr. John Oates himself and James Nance. Examining physicians were noted doctors of the day like Dr. W.C. Highsmith, Dr. Seavy Highsmith and Dr. R.L. Pittman.

With Fort Bragg being one of the only military installations of its kind, as well as the largest, its role in World War II was great. So many thousands of young men began pouring into Fort Bragg that neither the camp nor the city quite knew what to do. As Parker writes:

> *A temporary city of tents went up, and a furious barracks-construction program was launched. Soon, dusty country roads were jammed with columns of marching soldiers and armies of carpenters, plumbers, electricians, and other construction workers.*

In the first nine months of 1940, more than 30,000 workers built 2,739 wooden barracks, and yet Fort Bragg continued to grow. In June 1941, Fort Bragg was featured in a twelve-page photo spread in *Life* magazine, captioned, "With 67,000 men, It Is Army's Biggest Camp." By the end of 1941, that number had grown still. More than 90,000 troops were contained within Fort Bragg and Pope Air Force Base. In December, the nation was at war. Thousands upon thousands would soon embark for the warfront.

THE FAYETTEVILLE AND FORT BRAGG RELATIONSHIP

Since Fort Bragg's creation, there had always been a love-hate relationship with the city of Fayetteville. Thousands of people arrived seemingly overnight, but at the same time, businesses boomed and the economy was as stable as it had been in a long time. Without Fort Bragg, it's entirely possible that Fayetteville could have drifted away during the Great Depression, descending into the dusty sort of slumber that has affected so many other rural farming towns in the South. This sentiment is not necessarily shared by all, but when *Life* magazine published "A Sneak Raid on Fayetteville," the *Fayetteville Observer* came to Bragg's defense.

Life wrote:

> *Fayetteville is not a town loved by the men at Fort Bragg and the feeling is reciprocal. Soldiers have been known to hitchhike all the way to Raleigh, 69 miles away, and go to a movie that is also playing in Fayetteville, just in order to avoid seeing Fayetteville. On the other hand several of the restaurant proprietors of Fayetteville show their dislike and distrust of soldiers by demanding that they pay in advance when they order a meal and by giving them paper napkins instead of the cloth ones they furnish to civilians.*

The March 1942 *Fayetteville Observer* article retorted:

> *Here in Fayetteville we know that the picture painted in* Life *magazine is a distorted, inaccurate and unfair picture; but millions of readers of this widely-circulated and in many respects instructive and interesting weekly, have never been to Fayetteville to see for themselves, do not understand the problems existing here and accept the gratuitous canard as the whole truth.*
>
> *This is hurting Fayetteville now and will hurt Fayetteville even more after the war by creating the false impression in the minds of millions of people that Fayetteville is a greedy, hateful community that despises and mistreats the men in uniform who are training at Fort Bragg to risk their lives in the defense of their country.*

The article went on to describe how Fayetteville citizens should react to the *Life* magazine article:

> *We must not let this attempt of an outside publication to drive a wedge between the soldiers and the civilians succeed. It is true that* Life *has seized upon isolated instances and portrayed them to the Nation as representing the whole. We resent that.*
>
> *At the same time, we know that there are isolated instances of these things used by* Life *to brand the entire community. One of them is too many...We must consciously and conscientiously redouble our efforts to be pleasant and hospitable to the soldiers and to be sympathetic with their desires to find relaxation from their military duties while in our city.*

The effects of the war and of Fort Bragg could indeed be seen all over the city.

Military trucks can be seen parked outside the Town House in downtown Fayetteville, alongside a Coca-Cola delivery truck. *Library of Congress Prints & Photographs Division.*

WARTIME EFFORTS

Despite the largely negative and mostly false light painted of the Fayetteville and Fort Bragg relationship, both soldiers and civilians alike banded together during the war. As Parker writes:

The wartime experiences of those who stayed at home were typical of people throughout the nation. There were shortages and rationing, but farmers were pleased when prices for crops went up sharply. Hundreds of county men and women went off to good paying war-industry jobs elsewhere. Women who stayed home joined in Red Cross "sewing-bees" at the courthouse. They prepared comfort packages for shipment overseas. Families cultivated victory gardens, salvaged tin cans, and accepted the rationing that allowed them three gallons of gasoline a week and a pound of sugar a month.

Roy Parker provides a detailed list of the military units that heralded from Fort Bragg:

Among the units that went off to war from Fort Bragg and gained fame in battle were the Ninth Infantry Division, which landed in North Africa in November, 1942, stormed across Utah Beach on D-Day, June 6, 1944, and fought in Belgium and Germany. On D-Day, the famous original airborne divisions—the 82nd and the 101st—parachuted behind enemy lines on Utah Beach. They fought in December, 1944, in the "Battle of the Bulge."

It is not too far reaching to say that Fort Bragg (and subsequently Fayetteville) played a larger role in war efforts than any city in the country, as soldiers from its soil were present at the biggest and most important battles of the entire war.

At the war's end in 1945, the same Eighty-second Airborne that had been so pivotal in the liberation of Europe made Fort Bragg its permanent station, forever immortalizing the base as the "Home of the Airborne."

CUMBERLAND COUNTY VETERANS

Fort Bragg sent several thousands of men overseas to fight during World War II, though many of them came from other parts of the United States in order to start their journey here. There were, of course, native Cumberland County men who served, too. With little distance to go, and having been in the throes of Fort Bragg since its inception, Fayetteville boys felt a special sense of duty to their country. The adjutant general of North Carolina provided the following statistics about Cumberland County men who served during World War II:

> *According to our records in World War II, Cumberland County furnished:*
> *ARMY—White*
> *53 officers; 640 enlisted and inducted; 5 killed in action; 48 wounded in action; 5 died of wounds; 2 died of disease AEF, and 6 died of disease domestic or in this country. Total—759.*
> *ARMY—Colored*
> *341 enlisted and inducted; 6 wounded in action; 1 died of disease AEF; 6 died of disease domestic. Total— 354.*
> *NAVY*
> *11 officers; 96 enlisted and inducted. Total—107.*
> *It was estimated that the World War II veteran population of Cumberland County was 6,172, which includes all men and women from the county who served in any branch of the armed forces. A list of dead and missing of WWII published by the War Department in June 1946 gives 128 Army casualties from Cumberland County. The State summary of war casualties for North Carolina as published by the U.S. Navy in 1946 does not contain tabulation by counties.*

LIFE AFTER WAR

Because there was such a great population of soldiers hailing from Fort Bragg, there was a great deal of fear when the war ended that the resurgence in population was again going to shock Fayetteville's system. This worry was driven home with the realization that there might be an economic collapse since war-centered jobs were no longer needed.

Catherine Lutz wrote of this scenario in her book, *Homefront*:

> *The war's end affected civilian life in a variety of ways. The GI Bill, instituted in 1944 to boost morale as the war tore on, had perhaps the largest effect. With its support for veterans' mortgages, it helped fund the suburbanization of Fayetteville. It gave a great boost to the growth of several city colleges when its educational benefits plumped up enrollments.*

The population of Fort Bragg dropped after the war, as not everyone chose to return to service. Numbers fell to about eighteen thousand soldiers yet were constantly in flux until the millennium. Every military conflict in which the United States has been involved has affected Fort Bragg in some way, both large and small.

Fort Bragg has forever changed the culture of Fayetteville, both in negative and positive ways (though most would say for the better). Fayetteville went

A man stands in the arch of the old Town House, watching the hustle and bustle of a busy, happy downtown life. *Library of Congress Prints & Photographs Division.*

from a quiet mill town to a bustling military metropolis, a distinction that will remain with it for many, many years to come. The hope of continued success that Fayetteville citizens have lies in the city's heritage, in the ability to change the attitude of every soldier stationed at Fort Bragg through its legend, its culture and its long and colorful history.

Epilogue

FAYETTEVILLE TODAY
AND TOMORROW

Since World War II, Fayetteville's role in North Carolina and the United States has mainly been military related. Fort Bragg has become the largest military installation in the country in terms of population. (It is beaten in acreage only by Fort Bliss in El Paso, Texas.) The relationship between Fayetteville citizens and the soldiers of Fort Bragg and Pope (now Pope Army Airfield) has remained largely positive. Citizens of both have worked hard to come together in a way that mutually benefits the city. Fayetteville has even been named an All-American City twice by the National Civil League (an award given to only ten cities a year).

The All-American City Award is the oldest community-recognition program in the nation and recognizes communities whose citizens work together to identify and tackle community-wide challenges and achieve uncommon results. This distinction speaks volumes of the bond between Fort Bragg and Fayetteville, a once rocky and sometimes negative relationship.

In fact, Fort Bragg has helped maintain Fayetteville's economy through every recession since the Great Depression. Its military bases and soldiers keep the economy stimulated, keep consumer confidence high and have taught Fayetteville citizens and business owners how to handle fast-paced changes.

Fayetteville has been able to expand from a modest gristmill on the Cross Creek to a booming city—the sixth largest in the state of North Carolina—with a rich history and a vibrant future. Stories and legend exist on every cobblestone, in every brick of its historic buildings and in the grass and trees of its parks.

Change occurs daily, but a strong sense of self and a deep appreciation for roots keeps Fayetteville honest, good and hardworking. Through resilience and sweat on the brows of its citizens, it has bounced back from every major pitfall and hardship, making it stronger and stronger.

In the 1890s, Robert Cochran Belden, a beloved Fayetteville newspaper writer known to his readers as Senex, published weekly columns, providing anecdotes and stories for his readers. Belden wrote well into his eighties, and in his final article on September 28, 1893, he closed with words so appropriate:

> *In conclusion, let me say that as a son of this old town, I rejoice to know that her skies grow brighter. Wearing a new garb, with evidence of thrift and enterprise on every side, and iron horses prancing through her streets, she is like the bird of fable rising from her ashes.*

BIBLIOGRAPHY

Angley, Wilson, Jerry L. Cross and Michael Hill. *Sherman's March through North Carolina: A Chronology*. Raleigh: North Carolina Division of Archives and History, 1995.

Belden, Robert Cochran. *Traditions of Cross Creek and Reminiscences of Fayetteville*. Fayetteville, NC: The Fayetteville Observer Press, 1893.

Camp Bragg and Fayetteville: Sketches of a Camp and City. Richmond, VA: Central Publishing Co., 1919.

Cape Fear Valley Festival, Inc. *The Cumberland County Bicentennial Celebration Souvenir Program*. Fayetteville, NC: The Fayetteville Observer Press, 1954.

Codrington, Joyce. *Reverend Henry Evans*. Cumberland County Public Library and Information Center, February 1990.

Barnes, Greg. "The Great Depression: 'We Were All in the Same Boat.'" *Fayetteville Observer*, May 17, 2009.

Brandon, Edgar Ewing. *A Pilgrimage of Liberty*. Athens, OH: The Lawhead Press, 1944.

Denney, Robert E. *The Civil War Years: A Day-by-Day Chronicle of the Life of a Nation*. New York: Sterling Publishing Co., 1992.

Fayetteville Observer. "Foster Outlines Health Measures." September 1945.

———. "An Unfair Attack." March 16, 1942.

Fayetteville State University. "FSU History." Fayetteville State University Public Relations. http://www.uncfsu.edu/pr/history.htm.

Force, Peter, Allan Kulikoff and Northern Illinois University Libraries. *American Archives: Documents of the American Revolution, 1774–76.* Series 4, vol. 2. DeKalb: Northern Illinois University, 2004–5.

Graham, William. "Past Voices: Letters Home." Olive Tree Genealogy. http://www.pastvoices.com/usa/wmgraham63.shtml.

Gray, R.L., Jr. "Mrs. Roosevelt Pays City of Fayetteville an Unexpected Visit." *Fayetteville Observer,* March 5, 1934.

Greenbaum, Lucy. "Special to the *New York Times." Fayetteville Observer,* December 21, 1941.

Jackson, Claude V., III, Jack E. Fryar and North Carolina Department of Cultural Resources. *The Big Book of the Cape Fear River.* Wilmington, NC: Dam Tree Books, 1996.

Johnson, Lloyd. "Highland Scots." North Carolina History Project. http://www.northcarolinahistory.org/encyclopedia/110/entry.

Johnson, Lucille Miller. *Hometown Heritage.* Raleigh, NC: The Graphic Press, Inc., 1978.

———. *Hometown Heritage.* Vol. 2. Dallas, TX: Taylor Publishing Company, 1992.

Lutz, Catherine. *Homefront: A Military City and the American 20ᵗʰ Century.* Boston: Beacon Press, 2001.

Moffitt, Allene. "Soldiers Town Home." *Fayetteville Observer,* June 17, 1944.

North Carolina Museum of History. *Babe Ruth.* N.p.: Office of Archives and History: Legend Series, 2005.

Oates, John A. *The Story of Fayetteville and the Upper Cape Fear.* Charlotte, NC: Dowd Press, 1950.

Office of the Adjutant General, General Papers and Books. *General William T. Sherman.* Vol. 18, *Letters Sent, April 14–July 9, 1865.* National Archives, Washington, D.C.

Parker, Roy, Jr. *Cumberland County: A Brief History.* N.p.: North Carolina Division of Archives and History, 1990.

Porter, Dr. Joseph C. "The First People of North Carolina." North Carolina Museum of History. www.ncmuseumofhistory.org/collateral/articles/F05.first.people.pdf.

Powell, William S. *North Carolina: A History.* N.p.: University of North Carolina Press, 1977.

———. *North Carolina Through Four Centuries.* N.p.: University of North Carolina Press, 1989.

"Rates of Way—Freight and Passage Between Fayetteville & Wilmington."
Image. Online Special Collections Library, Duke University. http://
library.duke.edu/digitalcollections/images/eaa/B/B04/B0445/B0445-
lrg.jpeg (accessed December 20, 2010).

Sherman, William T. *Memoirs of General W.T. Sherman*. New York: Library of
America, 1990.

Smith, James R. "History of Clarendon Bridge." Personal research, 1986.

Sparrow, Prep. "Silent Years in City History." *Fayetteville Observer*, July 3, 1960.

Spencer, Cornelia Phillips. *The Last Ninety Days of the War in North Carolina*.
New York: Watchman Publishing Company, 1866.

Sprunt, James. *Chronicles of the Cape Fear 1600–1916*. Wilmington, NC: Dam
Tree Books, 2005.

United Daughters of the Confederacy, J.E.B. Stuart Chapter. *War Days in
Fayetteville, North Carolina: Reminiscences of 1861 to 1865*. Fayetteville, NC:
Judge Printing Company, 1910.

United States Department of the Interior. "The North Carolina State Capitol:
Pride of the State." Teaching with Historic Places Lesson Plans. http://
www.nps.gov/history/nr/twhp/wwwlps/lessons/61capitol/61capitol.
htm.

University of North Carolina at Chapel Hill. "Antebellum North Carolina."
Learn NC: North Carolina Digital History. http://www.learnnc.org/lp/
editions/nchist-antebellum/5351#comment-1891.

———. "Camp Bragg." Learn NC: North Carolina Digital History. http://
www.learnnc.org/lp/editions/nchist-newcentury/5113.

———. "North Carolina in the New Nation." Learn NC: North
Carolina Digital History. http://www.learnnc.org/lp/editions/nchist-
newnation/4347.

Webb, J.S., Jr. *The Atlantic Coast Railroad*. Public Relations Bureau of the
Atlantic Coast Railroad Line, n.d.

Wilson, Bonnie. "In 1789, Henry Evans Called City's 'Most Remarkable
Man.'" *Fayetteville Times*, April 14, 1989.

ABOUT THE AUTHOR

Emily Farrington Smith is a freelance writer and army brat who hails from Fayetteville, North Carolina, by way of Cincinnati, Ohio. She has lived in Fayetteville for most of her life and graduated from Fayetteville State University in 2008 with a degree in mass communication. Emily is passionate about southern history and loves getting lost in her hometown. She and her husband, Ash, live with their son, Bennett, in Haymount.

Courtesy of Marc Barnes.

Visit us at
www.historypress.net